For my children

Caoimhín

Tomás

BIOGRAPHICAL DETAILS

TOMÁS McGEOUGH

Tomás McGeough was born in Belfast at 6pm 19-9-61. At the age of two, he, his one-year-old sister Jacqueline, Father and heavily pregnant Mother moved from his Grandmother's home at Ardilea Street Oldpark Road 'The Bone' district of Belfast, to a house on the newly built Turf Lodge estate in West Belfast.

Tommy was eight in 1969; the year 'The Troubles' broke out in Belfast, and being a 'War Child,' guns and violence became the norm. Finding IRA kneecap victims was a common occurrence, but his first experience of murder, was at the age of 14. On an Easter Sunday morning during an IRA internal feud, Tommy and his younger brother Francis, stood at the front door of the family home and witnessed a man being shot in the head by a man using an Armalite M16 assault rifle. In his short story 'Dead Man,' he describes the scene of the man lying in the gutter with words such as, 'blood so dark, like ox-tail soup, and, 'the steam rising as the hot blood met the cold icy rain of Belfast.'

Tom witnessed most, and lived through all the major events in Belfast: The IRA hunger strikes, he was present at the 'Milltown Massacre,' and watched friends fall in and out of the paramilitary organisations, and prisons. Although, in his own words, "the ones who fell to the grave never came home."

Tommy became involved in the drugs trade, and in 1994 he served a short prison sentence in Belfast for the importation of cannabis.

From 1994, the IRA, under the pseudonym of Direct Action Against Drugs, DAAD, have attacked and murdered friends, acquaintances and a member of Tommy's family, in a purge against drugs.

In 1996 Tomás was again in prison. Seven months remand on a trumped-up charge for traces of cocaine on a mirror. The charges were withdrawn and the case thrown out before the preliminary inquiry.

In 1997 Tommy left Ireland and bought a public house in Birmingham England. Things were becoming 'normal' in Tom's life, until after nearly two years out of Ireland, a national Irish newspaper, The Sunday World, named Tommy as the man who inherited a multi-million pound drug empire after the death of a leading Irish drug lord. His photograph graced the front page. Then a week later, it named him as one of the 'seven deadly sinners' who run the drugs trade in Ireland, both these stories were totally unfounded and, untrue.

All characters in this story and the story itself are fictional

Any resemblance to past events or people living or dead are purely coincidental.

*I originally used the names of real people, friends of mine, past and present. This in no way implies that they are criminals or played any part in this fictitious story. The inclusion of their names is taken as a token of my love for them. To some for inspiration and to all for having the time to spend some of their lives with me. All names have been changed, in this revised edition, to save any confusion or embarrassment to those wonderful people, in the telling of this **fictional** story; but the love I hold for those friends remains the same.*

Another Disclaimer

After reading this story, some people have said to me things such as: "Oh I liked it when you did this or that."

So I have to say again that this is a fictional story and I played NO PART IN IT!

Now, if you want to believe that I did then also remember that I had a hand in the assassination of JFK, I was the third gunman on the grassy knoll, John Lennon and Marilyn Monroe. I also know what side the Pope was shot on… BBC1!

If you want to keep believing; anything you think is true is probably a lie and anything you think is a lie is probably true.

What I will say is that two of the characters are based loosely on my own personality (well as I think I have behaved at different times in my life) a younger and older version of me, if you like. If you have known me long enough you may work it out!

I'm definitely not Julie or Mary! I THINK…

Those who really know me know the truth.

Tommy.

PROLOGUE

Belfast 1974

"Come on to fuck Gerry, the Brits are in!" Joe shouted at me through our open, hall door and into the living room, where I stood at the fireplace, the gas fire making my Wranglers smell as I admired my hair in the mirror. I was cool. Happy Days and the Fonz had just finished.

"Gerard, don't you be throwing them stones!" My ma shouted at me as I grabbed my Wrangler jacket and put my studded belt in the second hole, nice and loose in case I had to pull it off quickly and smack one of them British bastards with it.

Me and Joe loved it. We were only fourteen, but in the summer of 1974 we started just about every riot in Turf Lodge. The wee girls loved us and the kids admired us, cos we were always at the front. We were two living, breathing heroes and the best looking two kids on the street, with our Bay-City-Rollers hair cuts and jeans worn at half-mast, up our shins.

The noise on the street was deafening as we got near Ardmonagh Gardens. The Brits had come in over the fields at the city cemetery, through the flats and down Ardmonagh. We were running down Norglen Parade, 'Our Street', to catch them at the corner as they turned it. Joe got the first ammo, a house brick, and threw it a couple of times at the kerb to break it up. Even quarters were still too big to get any power into the shot, so we broke it down more. The best stones to throw were the ones that fell off the back of the quarry-lorries, the ones used in the building sites for hardcore. You could hold about three of them in your left hand, and they were hard as fuck; if you hit a Brit on the head with one of them, he hit the deck.

All the 'Auld Dolls' (women) in Ardmonagh were rattling their bin lids on the ground and blowing whistles to let everybody know that the Brits were in, and me and Joe loved it.

There he was, that wee Scottish bastard with the ginger hair. I fuckin' hated him. He just kept on walking backwards, smiling at me as I got closer. I knew he was ginger, cos one day I got him on the knee and he hit the deck. His helmet came off and I stole it, but had to drop it cos one of the other bastards shot me on the arse with a rubber bullet. It nearly broke my arse; I'd get him back.

There was six of them. Ginger was the last one on the left-hand side and he pointed his SLR (self-loading rifle) at me. The bastard hated me too. So I attacked and couldn't hear the bin lids any more. I was in 'the zone', my own little battle fury. I threw the same stones over and over again as they retreated. Cowardly bastards! 45th Royal Marine Commandos, the same shower of bastards that had pulled my Uncle Tucker out of bed and beat him up before taking him away and interning him. Now they were running away from me. Wee Gerry, the fourteen-year-old nephew of that IRA man. I'd be in the Ra one day; I'd fix them.

Then they turned down Norfolk Parade and we had the advantage: we had the hill. I got closer and a stone bounced off his SLR. The bastard had his sleeve rolled up and I could see he had a Glasgow Rangers tattoo on his arm; he was a Prod too. 'I'm goin'a do that bastard!'

I ran up somebody's garden path and lifted their milk bottles. I got four and threw two to Joe who was having his own war on the other side of the street. He had them in his hands about two seconds and then ricocheted them off some Brit's helmet. Joe was a crack-shot. I missed that Scottish bastard with my two.

The entrance to the Falls Park was on my left. It seemed so quiet and peaceful and I could see The Coolers, the outdoor swimming pool. Uncle Tucker used to take us swimming; but nobody went there anymore.

That bastard was still smiling at me, his eyes were scared but he was smiling anyway. Fuck 'em I'll get closer.

"SNATCH SQUAD! SNATCH SQUAD!"

They sneaked out of the park and were behind me. The shout broke my tranquillity and I could hear the bin lids again and yer man was running at me and his eyes weren't scared anymore. I felt fingers run down my back as I turned, like a hare when a Greyhound is on it. And he was a man mountain, fuck me he was about six foot six and built like a tank; no hat or coat on, just a green T-shirt, combat trousers and track shoes. And he had this big, fuck-off baton in his right hand, and it just missed my head. Jesus Christ, he was nearly on top of me, and I had to run up the hill nigh.

I don't know why I did it but I turned right into someone's front garden and ran around the side of their house.

"Run wee lad, run!" A pretty, blonde wee girl shouted at me as she stood beside her mother who had a bin lid.

Fuck me if they have a fence I'm caught, and he'll kill me. Fence, my bollocks this was Turf Lodge; we were skint. I got to the bottom of the garden and jumped into the next-door neighbour's garden. I could hear the Brit shouting, "Stop or I'll shoot!" as I slipped and fell down the bank and into the stream, 'The Falls Park River'; but he didn't have a gun. The Brit slipped too and fell down on top of me. The bastard had me by the shoulder and I bit his hand; he let-go and I scrambled up the other bank. Then he grabbed me by the ankle but let-go again when I cracked him over the head with my studded belt. And then my belt wrapped around his baton and he was after me again, up the bank and along the fence, and he was catching me, and both of us were covered in mud. One of the Iron bars in the fence was missing and I was through it like that hare. And he was too big and I still had my belt.

"Fuck you ya British bastard Ye!" I taunted him from the other side and stuck my two fingers up as I ran away.
"I'll have you boy!"
"Aye. Fack aff, ya wanker ye!"

1

Conor walked the hallway to the resettlement office; he had an appointment with Julie Murphy, a probation and resettlement officer, who worked in the Offender Manage Unit (OMU), at HMP Longmoore, a minimum-security category D open prison thirty miles north of London.

It wasn't the first corridor he had walked this past few years, but most times he had been escorted by a prison officer or 'screw,' as they are commonly called by the population of the many establishments that make up the British prison system. The term 'screw,' was named after the punishment handed out by the officers in the 'Victorian' prisons of the late 19th century,where the prisoner was made to turn a handle on a box that contained stones and rocks for hours on end. A task that served no purpose only to take the skin and flesh off the prisoner's hands; sometimes the officer would tighten up the screw on the box, just to make it harder to turn, hence, 'screws.'

Sometimes Conor had walked unescorted with the rabble of men as they made their way to or from work or the education department, but there was always a 'screw' at the gate and others stationed at checkpoints along the route. Conor was now in open conditions and he had to find things himself.

He was coming to the end of a six-year sentence for the social supply of drugs, and having worked his way through the different security category prisons in the British system, which are: Category 'A', maximum security, which Conor felt lucky to have never experienced, as these are the places where you could quite easily become someone's 'girlfriend' or '*bitch*,' whether you liked it or not. Category 'B'; there are two types of B-cat, one is a local prison where remand prisoners are kept until they are sentenced and re-categorised before being sent off to their respective category prison. This type of B-cat is also a holding prison, for sentenced prisoners, before being sent off to their 'training' prisons. The other B-cat is a training prison, where sentenced B-cat prisoners are sent to complete offender behaviour courses, interventions and to gain education and employability skills. Category 'C' is similar to a B-cat trainer only lower security and this is where Conor had spent most of his sentence. Category 'D' is an open prison and the lowest security rating. Conor had finally earned his D-Cat and was here to be assessed while parole was being considered.

HMP Longmoore was unlike any of the other prisons that Conor had had the 'pleasure' of visiting, whilst on the national circuit, being sent to prisons all over the country; it was open and totally alien to him; no razor wire, no guards with dogs; and no locks. Each room had a single bed, a table, chair and a television sat on top of a chest of drawers that held your clothes. There were no bars on the windows; in fact, Conor had a view of trees and a lake, where members of the public could join the prison owned fishing club and while away the hours fishing for carp or trout. His usual 'Buena vista' was a fence, a wall and razor-wire. That was over now and Conor was happy about that. Prisoners were here on trust; lifers and white-collar criminals who were coming to the end of their sentences and waiting for the, 'time to go home.'

Longmoore had been an army camp, in its previous life; then after two of the many regiments of the British Army merged, the camp was handed over to the prison service and Her Majesties Prison Longmoore, was born.

The prison was still laid out like an army camp only the billets were now called wings, A-D and two units that held prisoners who had worked hard to earn their enhanced status on the Incentive Earn Privileges scheme. (IEP). These units were named after the prison, a play with words, Long and Moore units.

Long and Moore residents mainly worked outside the prison in either their own job or doing charity work, they only really slept there, as some of their licences were from 7am-7pm. They had one town visit, RDR (Resettlement Day Release) per week and a five day home leave, ROR (Resettlement Overnight Release) every twenty eight days. Conor was housed in the old billets, 'A' wing, the drug free wing that over looked the old parade ground, lake and the forest on the outskirts of prison.

Conor was a good-looking lad. Twenty-seven years old and had been in prison for four years; a year longer than he should have been because of a difference of opinion with a Governor in the first year of his sentence. Now an extra twelve months and an enhanced thinking course had been a bit of an attitude adjuster. He had been passing his time working-out in the gym and putting a bit of muscle on his six foot one frame. Conor felt good about himself, he had left the drugs behind and was back to the Conor, 'Jack the lad,' routine of old.

"Come in, the door's open." Julie called in an accent he didn't recognise, somewhere between Donegal and New York, mid-Atlantic. 'Maybe she's a mermaid,' he giggled to himself as he swaggered through the door; the chip had almost left his shoulder.

"I'm Conor Loughlin," he looked up and then stood speechless for the first time in four years of backchat.

Julie sat at a large, oak table with pens and pencils neatly arranged around a photo of a lilac Persian cat, the paper on the leather bound blotting pad had no doodles of flowers, she was much too classy for that: she had to let the men know she was serious.

"Take a seat." Julie pointed to a pink velour chair with no arms, her jet-black hair shone like wet tarmac after the sun splits the clouds and her eyes dark and sultry seemed to sparkle as the sun beamed through the bay window.

"Hello Conor, I've been asked to do this first interview for Mr Sharples, he's your personal officer, but he's off sick so I've been asked to fill in for him."
"Oh, OK."
"I work on the lifer unit so you won't see me that often, as I said, I'm just filling in."
"Jees, that means I have to talk to a man, I thought my luck was in." Conor teased. Julie allowed herself a little smile.

Julie was a private girl, a very beautiful, private girl, five-six and twenty six years old with long-flowing, shiny-black hair that would have had a loose curl in her teens but now it had dropped to a bouncy wave. If she had pulled it, it could have touched her tiny waist but let loose it bounced just below her breasts, which bounced also, when she walked. She had curved hips and long legs. She turned heads. Her deep blue eyes were piercing. Black eyelashes, long with a curl, batted; dark and sultry. They hid pain but longed for love. A college education in Boston Massachusetts had opened up her way of thinking. The USA and its in-your-face attitude was so very different from Bury St Edmunds Suffolk, where she had grown up, but a failed romance with a collage jock had left her bitter. All the plans they had had just got blown out of the water when he got a draft for the San Francisco 49ers.

Conor reminded her of her lost love, tall and handsome, with a fresh face, broad shoulders and an infectious smile. His eyes were dark, but the sunlight played tricks with the colour. Depending on the light, they could be blue or green, even dark hazel. Sometimes they seemed to change colour separately and his dark lashes hid the truth behind that smile. Conor said that they were lucky eyes; girls said that they were captivating. His hair had been fair as a child but now was dark brown, and he wore it swept back with gel. Conor had boxed in his teens, like most kids from the ghetto, but those big hands seemed so gentle. She read the signs as he spoke. Legs and arms open: giving himself; 'I've nothing to hide, I'm being honest.' Palms up gesture: almost submissive. She liked Conor. He spoke in an Irish accent, but not from the cities - not hard or harsh, but soft, almost a drawl; his words seemed to land softly, like the down of a feather bed.

"So this Mr Sharples, when will he be back then Miss Murphy?" Conor's words woke her from her dream.
"Miss Murphy, that's very formal, things are a bit more relaxed here in D-cat Conor, Julie's fine."
"Bet your friends call you Jules?"
"They do."
"So Jules it is then?"
"Julie *is* fine Conor," she allowed herself another little smile. 'Cheeky boy,' she thought, 'flirting with a member of staff.' She liked it, but could never allow herself to admit it, but she liked him anyway.
"You know I heard it's his wife who's sick and he's looking after her," said Julie.
"So you'll see a lot of me then? But only if you're nice." Conor liked it when Julie smiled.

"Now Conor, you've been brought to a D-cat prison as you're eligible for parole and to be re-assessed, basically, to get you into resettlement and help you fit back into society again." The conversation was more formal now; the flirting had stopped, as both knew the importance of what was going on. Julie spoke about how the resettlement scheme worked: risk assessment, the IEP scheme, the basic, standard and enhanced levels where prisoners are given targets to reach, the further up the regime they move the more privileges they get. Conor was more concerned about his private cash and did it arrive from the last prison?

"And when you finish your induction Conor, we'll sort all of that out for you."
"Thanks Julie." Julie was now on her feet and behind Conor, walking as she spoke. Conor's head turned as his eyes followed her.

This was not Julie's style; she was always so professional and spoke from her chair. It was leather and higher than the pink chair that the prisoners sat on. She kept the pink chair at the right hand corner of her desk so that she didn't seem too condescending. But this was different; she had this uncontrollable urge to be close to Conor.

"No problem Conor," she touched his shoulder as she stopped. Conor took her hand and stood up. For the briefest of moments they gazed into each other's eyes enchanted. He wanted her and he dared himself; then gave himself a mental slap, *'I'll get into trouble.'* She looked at him and she knew it; she wanted him and she wanted him to try; *'I'll get into trouble.'*

"I'll see you tomorrow at three Conor," They shook hands and smiled as he left.

2

Pat sat in the driver's seat of his own car. It wasn't the sort of car you would normally associate with a robbery, it only had two doors: a white Ford Escort, RS Turbo; and no-one in their right mind would use their own car to do a move but this was an easy touch.

"Any sign of it yet?" asked Dennis from the back as he leaned between the front seats, where Danny O'Neil sat flapping.

Pat had known Dennis Deveny since childhood. Dennis was thirty-four, medium build, 5'10 and the shrewdest man Pat had met outside of military intelligence. He was an armed robber, turned drug dealer and, coming from Dublin, was quick to give Pat a bit of work.

"No, not yet." replied O'Neil, his girlie voice giving a quiver.
Pat didn't like O'Neil: 'too slimy' thought Pat as he looked at him in a sideways glance. O'Neil ran his fingers through his bleach-blonde hair and fidgeted again.

'What the fuck am I doing with that clown?' thought Pat, but he had no choice in the matter: it was Dennis' move, and Dennis insisted that O'Neil was the man.
Pat ran over the play in his head once more.

(Yesterday 1.00pm Fox & Goose Pub)

"Pat, it's dead simple," said Dennis as they sipped from a couple of bottles of imported beer; "so easy *I'm* coming on the move myself!" He ordered two more bottles and flashed a wad of cash that could have choked a donkey. Pat's eyes lit up.

"Pat, you're in a bit of diff's with those drugs, it's cost you your job and everything, but this'll put ya on your feet again. I need a man like you who knows what he's doin' "
"What guns are you bringing?" asked Pat.
"None, we won't need them, it's only a kid in a flat receiving a parcel.
"What?"
"Well," Dennis continued, "I was talking with this pal of mine, he's only been started a few months in the drugs game; anyway off he goes to Belgium with this shady crew and seventy-five grand of his own money to buy ecstasy, the drugs being brought from Holland. Now this firm he got involved with, they're hairy as fuck: think nothin' of killing you; so the kid thinks he's in with a proper set of lads, until he hands over this cash in Antwerp and they send him on his way.
"No way!" said Pat, "Seventy-five big ones!"

"Yes way, my son; stitched him up good and proper. The kid told me he just knew he was never seeing his few quid again when he walked away."

"So where do we fit in?"
"Well my son, the kid knows where the parcel is going and all we have to do is go and get it."
"Where?" asked Pat.
"Ah, one of those council-housing estates, a shit hole; no problem."
"Carry on."
"Well what we'll do is sit and watch the flat. When the Post Office van arrives with the goods we watch the delivery and when the van leaves, we enter the flat, tie up the kid and exit with the goods.
"That *is* an easy one!" laughed Pat.
"Told ya! There's about twenty thousand e's coming, so a three-way split: me, you and the kid, and we'll pay O'Neil a wage.
"Who's O'Neil?"
"He's OK, he used to run with our kid, did a bit of weights with him, but I think he was more into the hamburgers," Dennis gave a laugh. "He looks a bit of a poof but he's a good driver; he'll drive the car when we come out."
"He'd better be Dennis, I'll be through that flat door in a flash, he'd better not fuck up the driving."
"Don't worry, it'll be easy as pie."

"Here it is now!" said O'Neil and woke Pat from his thoughts of yesterday.

"Easy boys." said Pat as the postman went to the side door of the van, then walked towards the front door of the flat with what looked like two shoeboxes wrapped in brown paper. Pat scanned the street to make sure all was clear.

Nothing looked out of the ordinary. A young couple with a dog stood chatting; two middle-aged men wearing suits strolled to work together; a young man in a tracksuit was jogging and a girl with a pram walked past a tramp, who lay with a bottle of wine at the corner of the street.

The postman knocked the door: no reply; he knocked it again: still no one answered.

"What's going on?" asked O'Neil, his heart working overtime.
"Fuck this!" said Pat as the postman wrote out a card, put it through the letterbox and turned back to the van with the boxes. "Change of plan lads, that bollox has our stuff, let's take it off him." At that, Pat was out from behind the steering wheel and in a few strides, was on top of the skinny postman who let out a squeal of surprise as Pat grabbed him by his collar and belt, and launched him into the back of the van.

"Keep your mouth shut!" said Pat, "This is a robbery. Lie face down, shut the fuck up and you won't get hurt!" The postman did as he was told and Pat grabbed the two parcels without difficulty. 'Excellent!' he thought as he ran back to the car.

The smile on Pat's face was so wide he could have eaten a banana sideways. Then he noticed the two men in suits running beside him. 'What the fuck?' One of the men put his hand out and caught him by the collar. Pat carried on to the passenger door dragging the suit with him, with suit two trying his best to get his hands on Pat; O'Neil was supposed to have it open, but Dennis and O'Neil were still in their seats, and the jogger sat in the driver's seat. Pat ran around to the back of the car, dragging the suit with him, and through the boxes on the boot spoiler. The suit's eyes rolled back as Pat landed a left hook and suit two turned into a rag doll as Pat bludgeoned him with what must have seemed like the proverbial cudgel but was really Pat's over hand right. The two suits fell into each other and for a second, stood like a pyramid, their weight keeping their unconscious bodies upright, then their legs gave way and they were on the deck. Pat ran to the driver's door to pull tracksuit out but fell to his knees when the tramp and the guy with the dog were on his back shouting, "Police! Customs!" 'Ah for fuck sake!' thought Pat.

***

"Conor, wake up, what's wrong with you? Did you get bad news at that meeting today?" Pat's words woke Conor from his dream of Julie; the prod with his fork may have helped also.

Pat was Conor's new friend, coming to the end of a sentence for robbery, another exile from the Emerald Isle: Dublin. Pat was forty years old, an ex-soldier and had served with the NATO forces in Lebanon. A bit of shrapnel was lodged in his knee: *'the morphine eased the pain, and the grass grew round his brain, and gave him all the confidence he lacked; with a medal of honour and a monkey on his back'*; hence the 5 years for robbery. That was Pat's story, but Conor didn't see any scars on his legs. Pat had a knack of changing the story to fit the situation; but it was not like you were going to get more time if you re-invented yourself. Pat was broad at the shoulder; his left shoulder had a tattoo of a snarling Pit-Bull Terrier with 'Who Dares Wins' written in a semicircle above its head, and 'Blood group A' written below its jaw. His time in prison had served him well, getting him off the drugs and back into shape. He was loud and aggressive but very kind and likeable, fair hair just receding and a mischievous eye.

"No, sound, have you seen that Julie Murphy?"
"She's a ball breaker, I think if she smiled it would crack her face, nice ass though"

Conor smiled as he thought of Julie, and Pat's words.
"They say she's a lesbian," said Pat.
"Who says?"
"They, you know they?"
"They say a lot don't they?" Conor retorted somewhat defending Julie.

"Fuck me Conor, she's one of them not one of us, remember kid it's always them and us."
"No Pat she's sound, you should have seen the way she..."
"What?"
"Nah nothing," Conor stopped himself. 'My head must be away,' he thought to himself.

Pat seemed to read his mind. "Is your fucking head away? She's only a glorified screw."

"I know, it's great isn't it?" Both of them had a good laugh as they finished their dinner.

At that they were on their feet and back in the queue to scrape the remains of their dinner into a large plastic bin that sat in the middle of the dining hall.

'That was a close one,' Conor thought as he scraped the last carrot into the bin.

"They always give you fucking carrots," said Pat.

"Aye, do you want a chocolate bar?"

"Aye", Pat made fun of Conor's northern accent.

"Then get the tea on dickhead." Conor slapped Pat on the back as he got up.

"Wait Conor, have a look at that!" Pat pointed towards the dinner queue where the latecomers were standing, waiting for the next tray of potatoes to arrive.

A young kid, about twenty-two years old and oblivious to the long-termers like Conor and Pat, stood there. He had clearly only been in prison for a few days, probably serving off a fine or a short sentence for a driving offence. He stood with his tray in his hands, his hair still showing the telltale signs of a perfect hairdresser's cut, not the Waltons-home-hair-cut-special, donned by most prisoners. His suntan had just changed to grey and he was swaying from side to side, about to faint.

"That's a cracker," said Conor, "another green about to hit the deck."

It's not a strange occurrence for first-time prisoners, who are green to the ways of prison, to be overcome with all the new emotions and stress and pass out.

At that, over the kid went and he was lying on his back, unconscious as the other cons stepped around and over him, not giving a shit. The prison officer who sat on a highchair, like the ones lifeguards use at the swimming pool, got on his radio.

"One down in the dining hall."

The Cons sat in silence watching the scene as they ate their food.

Now not much ever happens in prison but when it does it's usually hilarious.

Conor and Pat were giggling when Spud Murphy, an over-the-hill skinhead, got up and went to attend the fallen kid.

Now this act alone is totally out of character for cons, they usually don't give two shits, so the whole jail have now stopped eating, wondering what the fuck is going on.

Murphy, from the Greater Manchester area, was a street beggar; not a very good way to make a living? Wrong. Spud would tell stories of how he made £500, on Christmas Eve, at the Arndale Centre and he was getting around £300 a week during the year. What with inflation – it used to be: "Excuse me sir, could you lend me ten pence;" nowadays it was twenty pence and he had doubled his wage.

The law hadn't seen it so nicely. After the police had got sick of moving him along, he got arrested and received three months.

Murphy was streetwise and told lots of stories of life on the streets. He was funny, though he could be a bit of a nuisance sometimes and some people would treat him like the village idiot, which he most certainly was not.

So now, Murphy has the kid on his back and is giving him CPR. Everyone is watching, amazed, because Murphy, being a skinhead, looks like he's come straight from a white supremacist rally, and being an alcoholic didn't do him any favours into the bargain either.

Conor looked at Pat as Spud pumped away at the kid's heart and said with a laugh: "He's gonna kill that kid, he's only fainted."

Pat shouted across the deafening silence: "Murphy, what the fuck are you doing?"

Murphy looked up and shouted back, it's OK Pat, I know what I'm doing, I used to do first aid with Dr Shipman!"

Now Dr Shipman had just been found guilty of murdering two hundred, although the tabloids had it at more like two thousand, of his elderly patents by lethal injection, and the jokes going about the jail were about how Mike

Tyson had refused to fight the Doc as it was said he had a lethal jab; so the dining hall erupted with laughter and shouts of: "You fucking head-case." Then came an onslaught as slices of bread and cold potatoes rained down on Murphy. The kid woke up and started screaming.

Conor and Pat ran back to the wing, laughing, lads again.

Conor slept well that night, but woke early. Julie had been his last thought that night and his first that morning, 3 o'clock couldn't come quickly enough. He had a busy morning. After the induction he had to go to the kitchen about a job application. As there were no jobs going in the gym, the kitchen staff was the only staff who got to use the gym everyday.

He walked the corridor job app in his hand; the smell of this morning's cooked breakfast still lay stale and heavy in the stuffy air. It reminded him of the free school dinners at Gort ná Moná back home and the Christian brothers with the leather strap.

"Lámh, lámh eile", (hand, other hand) they spoke in Irish, while punishing you, 'sick bastards,' he thought.

The walls were breezeblock with a plaster skim and covered with many years of cream matt paint, with a green gloss dado strip. Grooves and crevices had been gouged into the plaster by carelessly pushed food trolleys, an empty one of which was parked up at the end of the corridor.

"I'm looking for Mrs Bronte!" Conor shouted across the din of the kitchen, men were washing carrots and pouring them into large steamers. 'Carrots again,' he thought of Pat's words and laughed.
"She's in the office," a short Asian lad with 'Mohammed' written badly in black marker on his cap pointed to a door, and in the process almost dropped his bag of carrots.

Conor walked across the kitchen shaking his head and smiling, 'carrots'.

The door was open so Conor casually walked in. "Ah, the door was open so..." he looked up and paused, "I'm here about the job." He handed her the app. Mrs Bronte wore a white coat and butchers hat with a red band. She had a bleached-blonde, shoulder-length, curly bob long due a refit, he could see that she was still in her late twenties by the skin tone of her arms, but she already had crows-feet through the constant squinting from cigarette smoke in her eyes.

"You're late!" she snapped taking the app. There was a loud crash as aluminium containers ricocheted off the floor. "What the hell is going on here?" she shouted as she made her way to the door, her cigarette still hanging from the side of her mouth. Mohammed stood with his bag of carrots, "Tell you what," she turned to Conor, "I'm up to my eyes in it here, start work on Thursday, be here at 6 am, you're on the breakfast shift."
"6 o'clock!" said Conor.
"And don't be late."

3

The ring of the phone startled Julie, three sharp rings then a pause, it was an outside call, internal was long and slow.

"Julie Murphy," she answered in her work voice.
"So when are we gonna do lunch?" The voice at the other end was taking-off Julie's accent.
"Simone, how are you sister?" she replied brisk and chirpy.
"Oh, I'm fine," still taking-off the accent.

Simone was Julie's twin, not identical but the resemblance was striking, although Simone was the more outgoing one, having dropped-out of college to join a pop band and dye her hair blue. Her hair was back to black now as she had twin daughters of her own, to the lead guitarist, now a Dr Frank Donnelly.

Simone was really happy with her life: house in the suburbs, BMW, high tea on a low table with the Farquars and Bishops. But the bright lights had hypnotised her and had showed in her personality. Now, Sunday afternoon karaoke was as far as it was going to go, and that was enough of the drug to feed the habit.

"I thought we were going to lunch Jules?"

"I'm sorry Sim, I've had so much work with Mr Sharples being off."

"Don't call me Sim," Simone cut in.

"Ohhhh-kay," Julie dragged it out, "Mom should have left the Sim out and just called you moan, because that's all you ever do: moan, moan, moan."

"So when *are* we going out to lunch then Jules?"

"Well it's too late today; I have this appointment at 3 I can't put off."

"You what? Can't put off, you mean *won't* put off. It's a jail for Christ's sake it's not as if they're going somewhere."

"This is different Sim…mone, there's this Irish guy I want to sort something for him."

"What! *You* want to what?" Simone was puzzled and intrigued, "carry on."

"No he's here by himself in a foreign country, just like I was in the States, and you know what? He looks so much like Lance."

"That dick head, you watch yourself girl."

"No, he's so gentle, he talks so softly. Anyway I *want* to sort this for him." Julie caught herself, 'what am I saying?' she thought to herself.

"Now listen Jules, you be very careful there. You listen to your big sister." Simone was always the boss; seven minutes had made her the dominant one.

"OK Simone, tomorrow at noon at Serendipity's Coffee Shop."

"Be there or be square." Simone took-off the accent again and hung up.

***

It was five minutes to three and Conor stood outside Julie's office in his best visiting clothes: a navy sweatshirt with Timberland in bold type across the chest, tight Versace black jeans, black Lacoste hiking boots and matching black belt. These were the remnants and his sole rewards from his drug career, but he thought he scrubbed up well and hoped Julie thought so too.

"Come in Conor," she remembered that knock from yesterday, four raps, one knock then three quick ones, Conor walked with a spring in his step, his hand outstretched to greet her. Julie shook his hand, she stayed seated always the professional but her heart skipped a beat as they touched. She smiled, pupils dilated and Conor subconsciously read the signs.

"Conor I've got to do a report on you for resettlement. We've got to talk about your past offending behaviour, victim awareness and a bit about your life back home in Ireland, that sort of shi... stuff. I know you've done your ETS (enhanced thinking skills) but this is just more hoops to jump through. I'll get you through it." Another big smile and Conor started to talk. He reminded her so much of Lance.

Conor spoke of his early life in Newry, Ireland, a small town, and how he helped on his uncle's farm as boy and youth. The days were happy ones until his cousin Kevin, who was more like a brother, fell into the slurry pit and it was three days until his body was found. Conor tried desperately to fill the void for his Uncle Kevin and Aunt Alish, but the pain of the loss of their only son was too much. Uncle Kevin died of a broken heart on Christmas Day. The farm failed and Aunt Alish went to live with her sister in Galway.

Conor left small-town Newry and took a job in Belfast as a butcher. Things were going well for him: he had his own flat, a little hot-hatch VW Golf GTI and the Belfast girls loved his accent.

One Saturday morning as Conor dressed the window he noticed a motorcycle pull up at the front of the shop; two big lads sat talking. Conor took a bit of interest in the bike as he had had motorcycles back in Newry. The bike was a Suzuki X5, a two-hundred-cc machine and Conor found it a bit strange for two big lads to be on such a small bike. Then the passenger got off and started walking towards the shop. Conor thought he recognised the man as someone who had tried to sell him a Toyota Hi-Lux the night before so he went to the door to greet him. At that the Greengrocer, who had the shop two doors away, walked between Conor and the guy with the helmet. Everything seemed to go into slow motion as Helmet looked at Conor and then back at Paddy again as they waved to each other, and then back to Conor.

Helmet put his hand into his jacket and produced a pistol. Conor froze. The first shot hit Paddy on the left side of his arse. The blood spurted out in the shape of a shuttlecock. Then things went back into real-time again as Helmet kept shooting. He grabbed Paddy as he fell and pushed the gun into his side. He must have fired nearly half a dozen rounds before turning and aiming a shot at Conor. It broke the window and lodged in the wall. Conor felt the ceramic tile splinters hit him on the back of his neck as he ran and pulled the rear door behind him. He thought he had been shot and decided that it was too dangerous to be a butcher anymore.

Next was a job as a doorman in a nightclub. This was how he became involved in the distribution of ecstasy. Most of the e's in Belfast belonged to the IPLO (Irish People's Liberation Organisation). Conor felt safe with his new-found friends, the job was soon forgotten as the money was with the drugs. Weekends lasted until Wednesday and things were going great until, after a few bouts of bad behaviour by uncontrollable members; the IRA (Irish Republican Army) executed their leader and other leading players. Three of which Conor had had the unpleasant task of pulling, dead, from a car that a bomb had been placed under as they sat drinking in a pub. Conor had been on the porch and said his goodbyes to them. The blast had punctured Conor's left eardrum and the sight of his friends, one with no legs and the other decapitated as the bonnet came through the windscreen was the deciding factor for a British Airways flight to London.

Conor was so much like Lance in looks and mannerisms, but their lives were worlds apart. Lance the big time football star; Conor had so much pain.

Julie's fingers wiped a tear from Conor's eye, her lips brushed against his forehead too lightly to be a kiss as she held him, then moved down his cheek. Conor turned his head, his mouth met hers and he closed his eyes, he could feel her body half on top of him, her hair brushing his face. He felt her heart pound and she felt his, his hand was trembling as he touched the back of her head. Her kiss was long, gentle and caring, then suddenly more urgent. She pressed her body hard against him.

***

The tinkle of the door chime startled Julie, Simone bounced through the door, the beep, beep, beep of her car alarm in the distance as she turned and hit the remote. "I always forget to lock it" she thought out loud, "Sister" Simone hugged Julie and kissed her on the cheek, the peak of her baseball cap almost hitting Julie in the eye as she casually threw her car keys on the table. Julie held her by the shoulders and returned the kiss.

"Hi Simone, you're looking very sporty, been at the gym?" Julie sarcastically joked. Simone hitched up the trousers of her powder-blue with the pink stripe Sergio Tachinni, fleece, track bottoms and puffed up the matching sweatshirt as she sat, "You know it, girlfriend" Simone came back in her very bad American accent.

"Can I top you up?" the waitress stood with a piping hot glass coffee jug, straight from the percolator.
"Thank you" replied Julie.

The hot steam licked Julie's jet-black curls and seemed to intertwine like fingers. The nutty aroma of fresh ground black coffee flashed her back to those brunch mornings, hot bagels, the USA and Lance, which triggered yesterday and Conor.

"Oh my god Simone, what have I done?"

4

Dominic took a deep breath, flashed his recently bleached teeth, nodded his head as if saying hello (the way pub singers and practitioners of folk music only know how), closed his eyes and let rip.

"…A*nd did it my way.*" holding the penultimate and last words as long as possible to milk every last drop of applause from the Sunday afternoon crowd, it was his show after all.

His almost orange, sun-bed, tan had been topped up in the same salon he had his highlights done. Simone laughed and applauded as he moved across the floor in his white stage suit, stopping only to shake hands with one of the punters who'd had a bit too much to drink.

"Great show Dominic, why'd you not get me to do one?"

Davie Wright staggered a bit then almost spilled his half pint of bitter and mild on Dominic's good suit before being escorted to the door by the security, who were always on top of their game.

"You look like your going to a Duran Duran concert." Simone teased and handed Dominic a gin and tonic.

"That man, I swear it's always the same thing with him every week, I just don't know why they don't give him his ticket and bar him; he's such a nuisance." Dominic replied in his camp voice and dabbed the sweat from his forehead with a silk handkerchief.

"He's a good laugh and he's part of the scenery round here. Anyway there'd be no show without punch."

Simone carried on laughing, and then became more serious as they took a seat facing a middle-aged couple that were still chuffed at themselves for giving their best ever rendition of 'Islands in the stream' by Kenny and Dolly. Martin still loved Cathy, his Dolly look-alike, after 30 years and 3 children. Cathy wondered if Martin was still able for the 'I'll get the blanket from the bedroom' routine, and settled for a half of cider instead.

"Dominic, I need to ask you about something, it's about my sister, you know the one who works at Longmoore"
"Twin, yes go on"
"Julie's her name, anyway."

***

"You did what?" said Pat, "What the fucks got into your head Conor? I fucking told you about her, she's only a glorified screw."
"Will you stop swearing dick head, I like her"

"For fuck sake. *Like* her? This is a fucking jail. You're letting your wee head rule your big head. For fuck sake Conor!"
"Will you stop fuckin' swearing; there you've got me doing it now."

***

Simone didn't feel as if she was breaking a confidence as she revealed Julie's story to Dominic. Dominic was like one of the girls. 'Who else can I talk to?' she thought. 'Being a doctor's wife can be lonely.' Frank was always on call and she could talk to Dominic, he was gay, he didn't want anything from her and she certainly didn't want anything from him. He was like the big sister she never had.

But he was still a man!

***

"Right Conor, I don't want to know the details."
"I wasn't gonna tell ya."
"Well you fuc.." Pat stopped himself swearing; 'got to sort this out' he thought. "You've said enough Conor, now listen, I hope you've only told me."
"Give me a break Pat, I know the craic, you're the only one I talk to."
"Conor we've got to be very careful here, this has got to be a secret between you me and her."
"Her name's Julie."
"You know I don't like her, but to be honest, that's probably only because she don't talk to me, but you know she does real good work for the lifers. Some of them bastards have nothing to hold onto, she gives them

hope. And me and you: well we're the only paddys in here; so those screws see us as a gang or something. If this gets out there will be trouble, and I don't want to go back to closed conditions, so keep your zipper zipped." Pat gestured as if zipping his mouth shut. Conor nodded.

***

'The flashing lights on top told them all that it was the cops, with the intentions of making a bust'

The transit van lay on its side in the field; steam pouring from its engine and a punctured rear wheel. Laser disks were scattered over the grass. The mud and cow dung camouflaged the pink graphics on the side of the van, which should have read 'Martini Karaoke - Anytime, Anyplace, Anywhere.' A Shetland pony lay with his back broken and Dominic sat crying into his pink handkerchief as a Police Officer accompanied the Paramedics and an officer from the RSPCA came walking across the field. A farmer screamed in the distance as he saw the carnage. The dead pony, the dressage fences scattered over the field and the legs of his little girl protruding from under the capsized transit van.

5

The summer was hot and dry and the days passed slowly for Conor and Pat. It just seemed so long to resettlement and parole. Put into perspective, it wasn't really that long, just after all that time in closed conditions they were like two kids waiting for Christmas.

Conor saw Julie every day and longed for her. She smiled but her heart sank and hurt because she could not hold him. Pat said that it was best for all.

Things were moving much faster for Dominic, 3 months had passed since the accident and because of a guilty plea he was fast tracked to the Crown Court, Crumlinville.

"It was a real shame what happened with that little girl Frank, I think I'll go along to the courthouse on Thursday to see what happens." Simone spoke with a deep sadness in her voice as she thought of Dominic, the gin and tonic and the dead little girl. She handed Frank his car keys and pager.

"I don't know why you're going to bother; it's going to be a formality. I know the doctor who did the autopsy. There was a closed coffin. He's going to jail." Frank kissed his wife, adjusted the stethoscope around his neck and drove his Merc back to the hospital for the night shift. Simone went and tucked in the twins.

***

"Driving while under the influence of alcohol is an unacceptable crime in our society. I take into account your guilty plea at the earliest opportunity so I must credit you for that, but a little girl has lost her life. So I have no choice but to make you a long-term prisoner. 4 years - take him down."

Dominic walked the stairs that lay below the courthouse and into the underground tunnel that went straight to HMP Crumlinville. One prison officer walked ahead of him, the other behind. The handcuffs looked so out of place on his manicured hands.

The damp, stone, paint-less walls of the tunnel made the air sticky and humid as it mingled with the heat of the hot water pipes that couriered the water to and from the courthouse and prison.

Dominic thought of the thousands of prisoners who had walked that tunnel before him since the Victorian days when it was built, some to the gallows. At the prison end of the tunnel there was another set of stone stairs, very steep that led to a steel door, on which one of the officers gave three sharp raps with his baton. As the door opened the noise hit him and wrapped around him like a blanket, as the ghosts of generations of wayward men embraced him and welcomed him to their world. The stench of ammonia and 'roll your own' tobacco lay heavy in the air. He thought of his good times in San Francisco. A man in a white boiler suit mopped the floor with an oversized mop; his handlebar moustache and shoulder length hair was like being in a time warp back to the 1970's. 'He must be a lifer,' thought Dominic. 'How in god's name am I going to get through this?'

***

Conor and Pat were engrossed in the News and Sports section of the tabloid papers. Pat was following a story of a schoolteacher from Canada who had been, allegedly, having sex with her pupils.

"Oh she's fucked now," said Pat, "she's only gone and admitted to kissing the young fella." Conor gave a sly laugh at Pat. He loved Pat's reactions to the story as it unfolded every day; he thought that Pat's reactions were more hilarious than the story.

"I don't think that Tyson fight will ever take place," Conor commented on the latest farce taking place in the crazy life of Mike Tyson.

"Jesus Christ, she's only gone and said that she had feelings for one of the girls also, and kissed her, but only as friends. Yeah right. *Lucky bastards.* Tell you what Conor; there were no teachers like that when I was at school. Lucky wee bastards." Conor couldn't keep his face straight.

"We went to single sex schools back in Ireland, you eejit, the only sex you where gonna get was by yourself, get it? Single sex." Conor motioned with his fist.

"Yeah those bleeding Christian Brothers, they'd have put a tail on ya if ya weren't careful."
"You're not gonna tell me that Brother Maloney was rootin ye nigh, are ya Pat?" Conor was going into a fit as Pat cracked him over the head with the rolled up daily paper.
"You cheeky northern bastard," said Pat; then cracked him again.

"Tell ya what Conor, look at this," Pat opened the paper. "Now he's a brave hairy arsed fif-fuckin-teen year old, and she's fuckin great." Pat pointed to the photos of the schoolboy with his face computer scrambled to hide his identity, and the photo of the schoolteacher, who someone must have sold to the paper as she wore a pink bikini and stood by the sea. "And she's only twenty four, for fuck sake. His Da should have gave him a few quid and bought him a pint for getting that one."

Conor lay across two chairs laughing as Pat carried on.

"And I'll tell ya what, if that was my son. I wouldn't have taken her to court, no way. I'd have sent the wee lad to school with a note asking her to call see me, to discuss the 'extra curricular activities' and help out with some pointers using my extra experience."

Another couple of lads had joined them now and all were having a good laugh.

"Yeah I read yesterday that she gave one of the girls a line of coke and tried to touch her up in the bathroom at the party. There's only one thing better than lesbian, and that's two lesbians." The laughter erupted again as Gary, a man in his mid-thirties from Cardiff, and serving a sentence for supplying cocaine, added his two cents worth in his strong Welsh accent.

"Go on Taffy, you're as mad as him." Conor was almost wetting himself. "How much did you get caught with anyway Taff?"

"Two fucking ounces, six years for two ounces."
"How much was that worth?"
"Well it cost me £1600, but they street valued it at £5000, I was only knocking it out for £2000, stupid dickhead me."
"Aye you'll not do that again." All the boys were still laughing.

"Oh you're right there boyo, I've got this man now, he has a fifty-ton hydraulic press and the right chemicals. He can do a bit of mixing and a bit of pressing and turn a kilo into two kilos. So even if you pay top dollar of £32,000 a key for 95% pure stuff from Columbia, after my man gets at it, it comes back 50% pure and that's good enough for the street and you've nearly doubled your profit. You get £25,000 a key every day of the week." Conor's expression changed dramatically and his mind flashed back.

Belfast 1994

"For fuck sake Conor, luck at the state of ye. You're in the movement nigh. You're supposed to keep an air of respectability about ye at all times. Them fuckin e's, they're for them fuckin' eejits dancin' there with their shirts off, rubbin' Vicks into their chest and blowing whistles like fuckin' headers. You're supposed to be lookin' after the dealers, not eatin' the profits. You're in with the big boys nigh gettin' a few quid for the cause. Nigh we're gettin' a good screw out of it ourselves, so stop you fuckin' it up for us. The IRA is already up our hole, they don't like all this drugs thing. Nigh this is the last time I'm coverin' up for ye. Luck nigh, I've a bit of different work for ye, only you and me will know about it, right? That way it won't go wrong, I'll be round at yours at 3 o'clock, all right?"

Conor got his dressing down from Sean O'Rourke, The O.C. (officer commanding) his unit of IPLO a renegade armed criminal gang masquerading as a paramilitary organisation. They ran prostitution, sold drugs and generally behaved bad. Although they did kill the odd solider, policeman and loyalist paramilitary for 'the cause' just so the nationalist people wouldn't reject them completely.

"OK, get me a couple of those e's before ya go, will ya Sean."
"For fuck's sake Conor." He shook his head. "Hey Micky, sort Conor out there. I'll see you the marra." Sean headed towards the door as Conor double dropped the

two e's, washing them down with a bottle of Bud, and pulled his shirt off.

***

Dominic's first night in prison was unlike any of the nightmares he had had. His only experience of incarceration was in the police cells. He thought jail was going to be like that, but at least now he had someone to talk to.

In the police cells it was just him, a toilet, a concrete bed with a two-inch thick mattress and a blanket. The constant shouting and kicking of doors by drunks and heroin junkies rattling for more dope almost drove him insane. He would have signed anything to get out. Now it was quiet in the basement of HMP Crumlinville.

Still, conditions were poor; he was kept three men in a cell, one single bunk, and two, one up one down. The walls had been freshly painted magnolia, but he could still read were men had scraped their names into the paintwork over the years. *Scully and Jim 1984 18 months wee buns yee ha.* 'Jail had obviously rehabilitated those two scally wags,' he thought.

He talked small talk with the other two he had been locked up with. One would only be in for five days to serve off a fine he hadn't paid. The other man in his late forties and who endlessly made and chain-smoked his role ups. He got three months for not paying his TV licence and kept going on about how much it was going to take to keep him in jail for the next three months.

"They'd be as well buying the licence for me. The story got a bit tedious but at least it kept Dominic's mind of his problems.

The next day after an interview with the governor, Dominic was taken to the wing it was long and clinically clean. The walls covered with the uniform magnolia and all bars and cast iron staircases were painted gloss battle green.

Dominic and the TV licence were given a bed-pack, plastic knife, fork, spoon and cup, then sent to the top landing where they were locked up till dinnertime.

The cell was cleaner than the one in the basement, it had two beds and an old Victorian writing desk that had it been restored, could have fetched a good few pounds. There were two chamber pots to urinate in, one each. The smell of stagnant urine mingled with powdered blue bleach that was given to keep them sanitised, or just mask the smell. 'That's where the ammonia smell came from', he thought. Dominic dreaded having to use it, 'what would I do if I had to do a...' Oh no!' he thought.

"Right make you way to the dining hall. Tea time!" came the gruff command from a heavyset prison officer, as he flung back the door not even bothering to look at the prisoners.

The atmosphere had really changed on the wing as three hundred men made their way to be fed; shouting and rattling cups on the bars as they walked liked ducklings after their mother.

Dominic put his plastic plate under the servery bars to receive his boiled potatoes, mushy peas and one dried-out sausage.

The pain took about three seconds to register, the hot water with what must have been half a bag of sugar dissolved in it, micro-waved, stuck to Dominic's neck and ear. He let a loud squeal as the pain was delivered to his brain with what seemed to be every nerve in his body, and just got worse as the melted sugar stuck to his skin like oil from a deep fat fryer. A large crimson blister immediately formed on his moisturised skin as his head turned to protect his face.
"Lock up child killer!" A prisoner with a bald head and 'Love and Hate' tattooed on his knuckles stood with a large blue plastic mug as two prison officers came running across the hall. Dominic dropped his dinner.

***

"Well Conor, that's the plan, we've watched their routine for two weeks to make sure it's all sound. Them Prods are moving in drugs through Securigroup, we've got an inside man who's making sure it's getting through for them, but he's getting greedy now and wants to fuck them over. He says there's a serious amount of cocaine on the wagon, I don't know yet what we're going to do with it, but we're gonna take it anyway and deal with him at a later date for dealing with them bastards in the first place. Anyway, so Thursday it is then, I'll come and stay with you on Wednesday night; I'm bringing McGuire he's on the job with us so we can go over the plan again that night."

"Marty McGuire, he's a psycho he'll kill the poor bastard."

"Nah Conor, there'll be no need for a clatter piece, (Belfast slang for a fire-arm) it's in the middle of the city centre. If the Brits or peelers see us on the way there, we'll get a tug, so we'll leave the guns at home, so to speak."

"Thank fuck for that."

"Right Conor, there's one more thing. Now only me and you will know about this...Mary McAuley."

"What about her?"

"She's a girl of yours."

"Fuck off she's a whore!"

"Listen, you're not saying that when you're ridin' her full of them e's after one of them raves, are ye? Ya boy ye!" The conversation lightened a bit as they both had a quick laugh then got serious again.

"After we get the stuff it will be hot as fuck. The Ra (IRA) would go mad if that turned up on the Falls Road. We'll put it to bed for a couple of days until the heat dies down then you get Mary out on Saturday during the day. Get plenty of drink into her and the key of her flat out of her handbag so as me and McGuire can get in without damaging fuck all and get the stuff under her floorboards till the boss gets a buyer on the continent."

"I thought only you and me would know?"

"Well, it's me, you and McGuire first anyway, and the boss for fuck sake, he's the chief of staff, it's his orders we're on. Conor we'll get a good cut out of this, know what I mean?" Sean gave a conspiratorial wink. "And when we get it dumped, I'll take a whack out of it for me, you and McGuire, fuck you can even give some to Mary, we'll have a good sniff and drink and maybe we'll all get a ride at Mary." The boys had a good laugh and Sean O'Rourke left.

There are four sets of underground toilets in Belfast; all are either in the middle or at the side of the road. One set of ladies and gents are in the middle of the road outside Belfast city hall, the others are at the Mater hospital, Shaftsbury Square and Tomb Street where the general post office is, and this is the one the three boys were watching.

Conor and McGuire stood with their backs to the toilet; they laughed and joked as if engrossed in a chance meeting with O'Rourke, an old school pal. Their OP (Observation Point) was around thirty yards from the toilets. O'Rourke wore a green Barbour coat with a matching hat that country folk wear when going for a walk. Conor and McGuire wore bomber jackets and baseball caps; all three wore blue jeans.

Sean O'Rourke looked at his watch and right on ten o'clock an armoured transit van, the one with twin rear wheels, parked up on the kerb, the opposite side of the road. After about thirty seconds the passenger door opened, the occupants were making sure all was clear.

A bald man with a beer belly in his mid-fifties got out and made his way to the toilet.

"Take your time lads; give 'em 'bout two minutes to get started." O'Rourke held back the boys who were now flying with adrenaline. "Right let's go."

The three of them jogged across the road, all the while looking around for signs of the police or army. There were none. The boys sneaked down the stairs. O'Rourke put a finger to his lips to remind the boys to be quiet.

The toilets were tiled with off-white ceramics long in need of a wash down and the trough urinal had brown acid growth caked to the corners that smelt as though it was first deposited during Victoria's reign. There was a strip of bubble glass bricks, the one at the bottom corner must have been broken in the 1960's as someone had drawn a 'ban the bomb' sign with black marker in the gap that was at street level. These were the only source of light.

The boys heard a whisper from the middle cubicle and O'Rourke pointed to Conor to go to the cubicle on the right. McGuire closed the toilet door and place two thick rubber door wedges to jam the door shut; nobody was coming in or out unless *they* wanted them to. Conor stood on the toilet and looked down into the target cubicle.

A teenage boy gave a grunt and a moan as the Securigroup guard penetrated him. The kid was bent over the cistern.

"Go, go, go!" Conor shouted as the guard looked up in disbelief. The door hit him hard on the back as McGuire kicked it in. The boy let out a scream as he felt his insides tear. McGuire punched the guard hard on the neck, just where it meets the shoulder knocking him to the ground and then gave him a good kick on his exposed bollocks just for good measure.

"Ah, don't hurt me Sean," the boy cried, petrified, as McGuire pulled him from the cubicle by his bleached blond spiked hair. McGuire gave him a bitch slap with the back of his hand and told him to, "fuck up!"

"There's no need to hit the kid," said O'Rourke, "for fuck sake I know his family." O'Rourke carried on. "Terry Hughes, you dirty wee bastard, I have a good mind to tell your Francie on ye. Your fuckin' ma would go fuckin' mad if she knew what you're at. Right boys get that other queer on his feet." O'Rourke was in complete control now. "Right Hughsy, you know who we are, you get into that bottom cubicle, wipe your ass and don't come out for another hour. If you say anything to anybody we'll blow the wheels off ye. Nigh fuck off!" The kid ran and locked himself into the cubicle. The boys sniggered as they heard him wipe his arse.
"Right you, ya dirty auld bastard ye. Are ye catholic or a prod?"
"A catholic," the man hesitantly answered.

"Gimme your wallet there," he paused, "Andersonstown Park." O'Rourke searched the contents of the wallet that the man had handed him from his shirt pocket and was reading the address from his driving licence.

"Right, we're the IPLO."
"Oh fuck!" said the man.

"Now we know where you live. We don't want *your* money. It's not *your* money we're after." O'Rourke handed the man back his wallet containing some cash, two credit cards and a photo of what must have been his family. "We want what's on that wagon out there. So I'm gonna hold on to this." He waved the licence in the man's face. "Any fuckin' about and we'll be at your door."
"I'll do anything you want," said the man, "as long as youse don't tell anybody where youse got me."
"You'll do what I say or we'll kill every one of ya, in that photo, do you under-fucking-stand?"
"Yes, yes, yeah!"
"We're not in the business of ruining your life anyway, just get that wagon open."
"OK!"
"Well get on to that fuckin' radio." The man got on to his radio and keyed the mike.
"That's a roger John, I'm coming out."
"Ten-four."

McGuire got the toilet door open and Conor walked behind the man up the stairs.
"Stop there," said Conor," "is there any Brits or Peelers about?"

"No, all clear," said the man.

"Right, just do your normal thing, get that door open, climb inside, we'll be in on top of ya. Make sure that yer man in there doesn't hit any alarms or we'll stiff the two of ya. ***DO YOU UNDERSTAND***?"

"Yes."

The man walked across the road stopping in the middle to let a minicab taxi pass which splashed dirty water on his uniform boots and blue polyester, with a red stripe, trousers. He gave two clicks on his mike and there was a loud clunk as the door was opened. The boys were now in control of the armoured transit.

Ten minutes later the transit was in Divis flats, a large complex of tenement flats that made most other ghettos in Western Europe look like Beverly Hills. The two guards were in the back with cable ties, acting as cheap handcuffs, on their thumbs.

Sean O'Rourke stood over to the rear driver's side of the transit as Conor reversed it under a balcony and towards some lockup garages. Conor didn't even feel the bump as the transit mounted the kerb and hit Mrs Nugent, whose son Patrick was serving a life sentence for the IRA.

The transit crushed her shin as the rear wheels went over the kerb, the woman's leg between the footpath and the road. Her little red tartan shopping trolley was crushed also. The two little wheels ran the length of the transit before being squashed by the front wheels.

"Fuck me Conor stop! Get that wagon emptied before someone sees what's going on." Mrs Nugent went into shock.

Friday

"Right boys, that's the last straw. Them IPLO bastards nearly killed Patrick's ma. They brought all sorts of heat into the area looking for that Securigroup van and they didn't even square us up. Take them outa the game." These were the sinister words of Spike Currie, OC, IRA.

Saturday

Conor and the lads sat drinking in the Plaza hotel with Mary McAuley. "Here Conor, slip them keys back into her bag and get a line of that up your nose." Sean O'Rourke slipped a small bag of white powder to Conor as the news flash came on the TV.

"*A man has been shot dead as he sat drinking in the Martin Sloan Republican club in Turf Lodge - West Belfast and a number of youths have been admitted to hospital with what are believed to be gunshot wounds to the knees. Unconfirmed reports suggest that the murdered man is Paul O'Neill - chief of staff of the IPLO. UTV (Ulster Television) will keep you posted as the reports come in.*"

"Right Conor, you stay here with Mary," said O'Rourke. "Make sure she knows nothing about that coke. Me and

McGuire are gonna pick up a couple of shorts (short fire-arms) and strike back at them Provos. We'll be back in an hour for ye."

Conor felt his eardrum burst as the bonnet went through the window of McGuire's car. "Conor, the boys!" Mary screamed as Conor held his ears. "What are we gonna do Conor?" Mary carried on.
"I don't know about you Mary, but I'm fuckin' off."

***

"You all right Conor?" Pat hit Conor another crack with the rolled up daily tabloid.

6

Dominic sat on the edge of his bunk sobbing, nursing his pride as much as his scalded neck, which was pink and tender, the blister having burst when the nurse touched it with the antiseptic cream.

A lint bandage packed heavily with cold cream covered the wound, which was pitted with little brown craters where the sugar had caramelised and melted into his flesh like chocolate chips on a cookie.

"Why me?" he thought out loud as he held his head and what was left of his pride. The walk back from the medical block was a nightmare; the wing erupted with 'nonce,' as he came back on. His neck stung again as he turned to hear them shout.

"Look Dominic, I can't even be seen to be talking to you any more." TV licence spoke as he paced the cell smoking his roll ups and shaking his head. "The rumour is that you nonced up the kid before you killed her."
"Nonce, what does that mean?"
"You know, nonce, child rapist, sex offender."
"Oh no," Dominic carried on, "it was a car accident; it was in all the papers."

"Dominic, this is how it is. They see you walking about with your fake tan and highlighted hair, looking and talking like a right poof. Then they hear that you have killed a little girl. They don't care about the facts; you don't fit into their world. You'll have to go on to the protection wing."

"What's that?" Dominic's neck stung as he looked up.
"That's where they put the nonces...eh...sex offenders so they don't get hurt."
"But I'm not a..."

"Doesn't matter Dominic." TV licence cut him in mid flow. "No-one will listen to a word you say. Anyway you'll be safe there until you get moved to a 'D' cat."

"Yeah the Governor says in about a month or two."
"Well that's it then, get on that bell and get yourself moved before the doors open again."
Dominic pressed the bell and waited by the door.

***

Julie sat sipping her freshly percolated coffee, as she glimpsed at a folder that contained the file of another lifer who had an appointment to see her that morning. Her eye caught sight of Chucky, the lilac Persian tomcat she had left in Boston. She took the photo and smiled. Chucky had been a birthday present from Lance. She remembered him as a kitten, just a ball of blue-black fluff, and Mrs Bernstein's warning that if she wanted to keep the kitten he had to be de-clawed and neutered.

She did not want any crossbreeding with her show Siamese.

Mrs Bernstein owned the large three-story town house in which Julie had had a flat in the converted ground floor. The house was in Malden Mass and just five minutes from the T, the underground railway system similar to the tube in London or the subway in New York.

Malden was free of the hustle of Boston and was convenient to get to and from the University and The Purple Shamrock Irish bar in which she had worked weekends to supplement her income. That's where she met Lance.

Julie looked at Chucky and remembered how he had no claws to defend himself, and had to be kept inside at all times. She remembered how being neutered had made him so gentle, the opposite of Lance, the soon to be famous football star.

'Maybe it was fate,' she thought, 'Chucky being bought for her by Lance, who she met in an Irish bar. Chucky, a big gentle pussycat, just like Conor. It was time to put Lance, Chucky and the USA behind her.

Julie swallowed hard and put the photo of Chucky face down on the desk. Then removed it from its frame, gave it a little kiss, placed it in a brown paper A4 envelope and filed it under C.

"Julie Murphy." The phone rang its three short rings and then a pause: an outside call.

"Hello Jules, it's Simone."

"Hi there, what's happening?" Julie switched back to sister mode.

"Same as usual, I just called to say hello and see if you wanted to go for lunch."

"Sure, no problem," said Julie.

"Oh Jules, there is one other thing."

"Carry on." Julie suspected a favour was about to be asked.

"Do you remember my friend Dominic, the one who had the accident and killed the little girl?"

"No I don't know him, but I vaguely remember the story."

Simone went on to explain that it had been six months since Dominic went to prison and she hadn't heard from him. She said that she had bumped into Dominic's sister, by chance, and that she had told Simone that Dominic was being moved to Longmoore.

"Is he a lifer?" Julie asked. Simone told her that he had received four years and asked if Julie could ask him to write or phone her.

"I'm on the lifers unit Simone, so I won't see him, but I'll leave a memo with his personal officer. OK?"

"Thanks Jules, you're a diamond. So I'll see you at Serendipity at about one o'clock?"

"OK, one is good. Serendipity, that's a funny name for a coffee shop. I had a hard time finding it the first time we met there, you know. And the strange looks I was getting when I said its name asking for directions."

"Yeah Serendipity," Simone spoke excitably as she told the story of how the shop got its name. "It means 'pleasant surprise quite by chance.' I know the girl who owns it. Her husband bought it for her as an anniversary present, I think someone owed him money and he took it as a dept, It's really just some-where she can meet with her friends and gossip. Anyway, she thought it was a pleasant surprise and called it Serendipity."

"I wonder if mum thought it was a 'serendipity' when she had us two?" The twins shared a laugh, said their goodbyes and hung up.

7

Longmoore was like a breath of fresh air for Dominic, the freedom was hard for him to get used to, but he was sure he would get by. And the gym, he'd get on remedials and lose some of that weight; so he'd be in the gym everyday with the kitchen staff.

Dominic used the rowing machine. There were three of them all beside each other facing the wall, which was covered in mirrored glass. Real glass, not that plastic compound they use in closed condition prisons in case someone decides to break a mirror and use the jagged edge as a knife. The plastic stuff doesn't brake or when it does it shatters into pieces, useless for nothing except sweeping up and has this strange annoying quality of making you look huge or skinny depending on how close or far you are away from it.

But this was D-cat, trust and real mirrored glass. Dominic could watch himself pull on the handle of the rowing machine and if he was sneaky enough he could watch the men behind him working out.

He noticed one guy in particular, pose bodybuilder style with his shirt off and wearing nothing but a pair of high cut black shorts that made his waist look tiny. He could see that in his youth the lad's hair had been blonde and he noticed those eyes. 'All he needs is a golden suntan,' Dominic thought, 'his body is fantastic'.

As the guy put his clenched fists on his hips and spread his huge back muscles, he got a slap on the ass by a bigger man who Dominic knew now as Pat the gym orderly.

"Get your shirt on skinny," Pat joked with the guy. "You need a good feed". Dominic thought that they must be friends and then gave a little "aheem" as he seen the slap on the ass.
"Yeah, right," the other guy seemed to retort in a softer but still foreign accent then started laughing and lifted his vest.

Dominic finished his fifteen minutes on the rower and decided to talk to the younger guy.

"Excuse me, I'm wondering if I'm doing' this right?"
"What's that," said Conor.
"I'm trying to lose some fat, am I doing' this for long enough?"

Conor went on to explain the principles of fat burning, how he should be working out at 65 - 75% of his maximum heart rate for at least thirty minutes. He went on to explain that since he was not that fit, it would take a bit of time to reach that target.

"Thanks very much, my name's Dominic." Dominic put out his hand to shake.

"Locky, that's my name." Conor felt uncomfortable shaking his girl like hand.

"Where you from?" Dominic tried to carry on the conversation but was cut short by Pat shouting across the gym.

"Yo, Locky." Pat was laughing and gesturing with his arms for Conor to come over to him.

Conor left Dominic and as he got to Pat, Pat grabbed him in a head lock.

"Oh, Locky is it, looks like you got yourself another girlfriend there stud."

Conor tried to wrestle back but the giggles had taken his strength away.

"Let me go, ya fag, you soldiers are all fags anyway."

Pat gave him a slap on the top of his head and let him go.

"Locky is it?" said Pat.

"Well I wasn't gonna tell him my first name, his next question might have been where could he get himself a job doin' a bit of manhole inspecting?"

Pat sat down laughing and told Conor to 'Fuck Off'.

Conor lifted his towel and headed for the showers.

Conor took his towel from the chrome rail as he turned from the room he didn't even notice Dominic standing there naked but for his socks.

"Well, Locky, what do ya think, will I ever get you...er...like you?"
"Ah, for fuck sake." Conor was having none of this.

Dominic smiled as Conor walked naked across the locker room; he felt a numbing thud and a blue flash as Conor's right fist struck him in the eye. The back of his head slapped hard against Pat's chest as he caught him on his way to the floor.

"Fuck's sake Conor, there's no call for that," Pat gave off," get yourself dressed and get out before one of them screws find out." Conor lifted his clothes and left.

***

"What happened Pat?" Conor was anxious to find out the aftermath of the day's events.
"Well that was pretty mad Conor. The PTI (Physical Training Instructor) screw came in and saw Liberace sitting there bollock-naked with his eye all red and swollen and me telling him to keep his fuckin' mouth shut. He must have thought it was me who hit him for not givin' me a blowjob." Pat tried to lighten the situation but Conor was too hyped up.

"What do you think will happen Pat?"

"Fuck all, he has to see the governor in the morning but I have him well pal'd up and wired off to say fuck all. He thinks I'm his best mate now. You're a dickhead for doin' that Loughlin."

"So you got it sorted then mate?" Conor laughed mischievously whilst rubbing his hands together.
"That was some punch you hit him wasn't it?"
"Aye, a cracker."
"Get the tea on ya boy ye."

Dominic didn't have a good night, he tossed and turned and his eye stung, but most of all he was angry with himself. He might be gay but he was still a man. That's twice he'd been hurt since he came to prison and he didn't deserve any of it. Conor seemed so nice, 'all he had to do was say no and I would have left it at that.' Dominic tortured himself, 'and big Pat, Michael, he turned out to be the nice one. I don't care, I'll not say a word to the governor, Michael's alright but I'll get my own back on that Conor.'

Dominic walked the corridor from the Governor's office dabbing at his eye that now had crustaceans in the corner where it had been constantly running. He passed another office door that was open about a foot and a half. He didn't look in as he passed but saw something in his peripheral vision that didn't register at first, or maybe it did, maybe his brain processed it and rejected it as being impossible. It took a few seconds for him to catch on as he turned to try and make sense of what he was looking at. 'Simone?' he thought, 'how could she be sitting in the prison dressed like a lawyer talking to a con?' Then it hit as hard as the punch from Conor...SIMONE...TWIN...JULIE...IRISH GUY...'Oh my God, isn't this just so dandy.'

8

The library was quiet, just a couple of lawyers that had been convicted of fraud sat deliberating. Their crime was knocking on people's doors on council estates', taking down details of what was wrong with their homes and promising to take the council to court to get their repairs done. The legal aid forms were signed, but that was the last the people ever heard of the property being fixed until the police called to tell them their names had been used in a multi-million pound fraud.

They were browsing through the legal books looking for loopholes for an appeal against either their or someone else's sentence; who they were probably charging something like a few ounces of tobacco or a handful of phone-cards; such is the currency in prison. They were totally oblivious to the conversation Conor was having with Gary, the assistant librarian.

"So this man of yours Gary, can he really re-press the Coke then?"
"No problem, I've even seen him do it. It comes back as hard as you like and he even puts a stamp on it like it's straight from Columbia."
"Shit, that's great Taffy."

"Why Conor, have you got something in mind?"

"Well I'll tell you what it is. Nigh Gary if you're not for real and this gets talked about it could get very messy."

"Behave yourself boyo, all everyone wants is a good few quid."

"Fuck it," said Conor, "I'll just have to trust ya. I have this man back home; he's actually a cousin of mine."

Conor was lying, but it's not like there was a rule against it, it was expected to keep your back covered. "And he has anything from fifty to seventy-five kilos of pure cocaine and can do with it being re-pressed."

"And this cousin of yours, can he move that amount of stuff?"

"Well, he'll give it a good shot once he gets it re-pressed."

"Would your man sell the job-lot for a good bit of profit Conor, it would save a good bit of fucking about."

Conor was shocked at that comment. "I'm sure he'd need about a million quid for that amount, who'd have that kind of money?"

"What? That's nothing to my man, he's well fat with cash, but twenty grand a key is pushing it a bit." Gary thought for a few seconds, "Now if there were seventy-five, that would bring your price back to about fifteen grand, and already in this country, I think he'd go for that."

"Well, no matter what, it would be brought into England." Conor felt his stomach flutter at the thought of a million pounds.

"Right well that's sound," said Gary, "I'll speak with him tonight on the phone, I'll speak in code, he'll know the score and give me an answer straight away. When can this happen?"
"Well I've gotta bit of time left to do here, but for that kind of money I'll walk outta that door right now."

Gary gave a little smile; he now knew who the cousin was.

***

The visiting area was quieter than usual. It was Tuesday and most of the visiting traffic had been through at the weekend. It was a large room with pink and blue velour chairs; four sat around each of the twenty low coffee tables. There was a little shop that sold tea, coffee, and a selected range of sandwiches and biscuits. If you were lucky you might have been able to buy yourself a hot sausage roll and a cup-a-soup. At the bottom of the hall there was a television set which played videos of children's favourites: Barney, Tellytubbies and Power Rangers. A few plastic building blocks lay scattered around; this was the children's play area.

Two prison officers sat at the other end of the hall where they could watch the room and to their right the wooden benches outside on the patio, where on sunny days the prisoners could sit with their visitors.

This is where Dominic sat with Malcolm, a man in his early fifties, slim build, grey hair, and about 5'10" tall. Malcolm wore a brown pair of brogues with a brown belt that complemented his dark olive green three-piece suit, a cream shirt and a tie that was fitting for a Member of Parliament. Malcolm was an elected representative of one of the boroughs of London and socialised in the trendy gay bars that Dominic was so fond of.

Malcolm was a married man with grown up children, but Dominic had been a 'special friend'.

"It's good to see that you've been moved to a D-cat Dominic, but what in God's name has happened to your eye?" Malcolm handed him his handkerchief, "And your neck, what is going on?"

"This is too much Malcolm. I want to go home." Dominic told the story of Crumlinville and how Conor had hit him.

"Well I did my best with the home office to get your D-Cat pushed through fast for you Dominic, but I don't see what else I can do for you."

"Well I know something. Maybe if you give them this, I can get some time off. Take me to a non-parole sentence and I could get tagging." Dominic told the story of Conor and Julie.

"Well," said Malcolm, very 'matter of factly,' "I'll take it to a friend of mine, see what he says, but I can't promise anything."

Dominic was so grateful; he wanted to kiss Malcolm as they shook hands

.

"I'll see you when you get out," said Malcolm, "you owe me one."
"Only one," said Dominic.

***

Another conversation was going on but this time it was in the centre of the visiting area, just past the fish tanks; where very nervous carp sprinted up and down the tank every time a child rattled the glass with a plastic brick.

"So this kid Conor, he must have the coke or be planning to steal it off someone, what do you think Gary?" The words came from Spooner, Gary's *man*; the man with the press and the money. He was a man of his mid-thirties, 6'2", and had boxed as a kid. Spooner lived and looked like a coke dealer, designer clothes, heavy gold chain on both wrist and neck and a gold Rolex sub-mariner, the one with the blue face on his left wrist. On his pinkie finger was a two-carat diamond solitaire ring. With his dark hair and complexion he looked straight out of a Godfather movie or maybe just 'Gangsters 'r' us.'

Spooner was a very cunning and dangerous man and Gary knew it.

"I don't know which one mate. He's been in jail a few yurs, but he says he'll go get it now."

"Listen Gaz," Spooner got really serious. "This is not my usual form, I'm a business man, I look at things in the long term, but this kid's a one off, he's not gonna be able to supply *us* every week." Using the word 'us' made Gary feel part of the gang. That's how Spooner wanted him to think. "Do you think we could take it off him?" Spooner already knew what way it was going to go down but was giving Gary enough rope to make him go through with the plan.

"I've already spoke to him about it, he's well clued up, he'll want to see and check the money before we see the coke."
"That's no problem, we can bring the money. Once he shows the charlie, it, and the money will be going back with us. Call it on!"

***

The look of shock and surprise ripped through Malcolm's face as he and a friend from the home office ran Conor's name through the Special Branch computer.

"A terrorist? How the hell did he get through the net for D-cat? He has red flags against his name." Fitzgerald, the man from the home office was trying to reason with himself. "Oh he's in for drugs, that wouldn't warrant a Special Branch search."

"What about Dominic and Julie Murphy?" asked Malcolm.

"Julie Murphy, she'll lose her job, she might as well go back to the USA because she'll never work here again."

"Dominic, what about Dominic?" Malcolm pressed for an answer.

"Dominic? Promise Dominic everything until we sort this out. But he's getting nothing, you've done good enough by him, he only got four years for Christ's sake for killing a child. Her father pays big taxes and he's still screaming, we'll be lucky to get Dominic parole."

Malcolm nodded his head accepting the fact that Fitzgerald was right.

"Now Conor Loughlin, he's a different matter, the Firm *needs* to know about him."

***

The phone rang long and slow and Julie went into work mode for an internal call. "Julie Murphy." It was five minutes to four on Friday and she hoped it wasn't going to tie her up for the weekend.

"Hello Julie, its Dennis Sharples." He spoke in a low and husky voice that is acquired from forty years of cigarettes and strong liquor.

"Hi Dennis, what's happening?" Julie was a bit surprised, Mr Sharples wasn't one for casual chat, in fact, it wasn't very often that they would speak during working hours. They were from different departments.

"Julie, I was talking with Mrs Sharples…. June. We never did get to thank you for taking some of that work for me when she was sick"
"It was no problem Dennis."
"Julie, June and I would like you to join us for dinner tonight; she wants to thank you herself."
"It's a bit of a short notice Dennis I've…"
"She's making that nice meatloaf you like so much," Dennis interrupted.

Julie liked the Sharples. They were a couple in there mid fifties. June had had a hysterectomy early in the marriage and looked on Julie like the daughter she would love to have had. Although she kept a bit of weight on, she was always poorly.

Both of them were from middle class families and spoke very prim and proper. June wore her sensible clothes and donned a blue-rinse.

Julie had met her at an office party and had been back at the house for dinner and parties.

"OK," said Julie, "but I can't stay all night, I've got to see someone."

"That's great Julie, June will be so pleased, and Julie I've something really important to talk to you about. It's *really important.* You need to hear it. So I'll see you at eight o'clock."

"Eight it is then," said Julie, then hung up.

The drive to the Sharples home took about twenty minutes. The drive was quick, it was mostly motorway, and Julie wondered what the concern was in Dennis' voice. 'What was so important that he had to talk to her tonight?'

The road rolled out in front of her, shiny and wet, like hot candy on a toffee apple. It had just rained. Julie put her wipers on intermittent; the left one squeaked and left a white mark on the windscreen, as it should have been replaced at the last service. Then she had to use the wash wipe as she passed a truck on its way to Dover. The driver flashed his lights to let her know that it was safe to move back in.

"Hello Julie it's so good to see you," June Sharples welcomed her with an embrace and a kiss on the cheek.

"And you June, you're looking well. How do you feel?" Dennis could hear the usual woman talk as he fixed himself a Jack Daniel's and ice.

Dinner went as dinners do and Julie waited patiently for the *important* something that Dennis had to talk about. Mrs Sharples made some excuse to leave the room and Dennis sat on the end of his chair.

"Julie."
'Thank God,' Julie thought. She had been getting anxious and Dennis knew it.

"I've got something to warn you about. I've been at odds with myself all day trying to find an easy way of telling you and there just isn't one. So I'm going to give it to you straight." Dennis took another sip of his Jack Daniels.

Julie was dumbfounded when Dennis told her what was being said in the governor's office that day, he knew all about her and Conor. 'That was nearly six months ago,' she thought.

"Julie, I'm not going to try and judge you, I've been in this job for twenty-five years and worked in women's prisons also. Anyone who says that they don't fall for some of the prisoners is a liar. Their world is a world we only briefly touch. There's something primal and exciting about them. I've felt love, lust and hate but I was always able to differentiate between the fantasy of it all and the real world outside."
"Fantasy?" replied Julie
.

"You see Julie, we're just normal people, the closest any of us come to danger is on a day visit to the zoo, but some of them are wild, untamed, with no sense of respect or regard for society, and in some cases even for human life. In there they are vulnerable, they look to us, we're in control. And that Julie...can be the attraction on both sides."

"What now?" asked Julie.
"Julie, come Monday morning the governor's going to suspend you pending a full investigation and Loughlin is getting shipped out."

"Oh my god!" said Julie.

"Julie, I'm putting my job on the line by telling you this but you only have one option."

"That is?" Julie was now pacing the floor.

"Julie, if you're suspended this will hit the newspapers. You have to get in there tomorrow morning and hand in your resignation. It's the only way to save face. Then they can't touch you."

June Sharples stood in the doorway with the coffee.

9

A large new building with dark glass windows stands on the south bank of the river Thames in London at Vauxhall. It is Vauxhall Cross, home of what the press call MI6, but which is actually the Secret Intelligence Service; SIS, (The Firm).

In an office in one of the upper floors, two members of The Firm sat in dark suits drinking coffee and discussing the future of Conor Loughlin.

"Conor Loughlin," said Simpson, a man in his late fifties with a baldhead and an Oxford education, "he was seriously involved in that incident in Belfast with the IPLO and that cocaine."

"The file is still open on that one," said Dixon, in her Cambridge accent, a thirty-five year old woman who had worked her way up from the civil service. "How are we going to deal with it?" she carried on.

"Well after the IRA killed most of the main players, Loughlin just seemed to disappear and the cocaine never emerged on the street. Loughlin is probably the only one who knows what happened to it."

"We don't want that hitting the streets," said Dixon.

"No, it's either destroyed or buried somewhere, and I aim to keep it that way." Simpson paused as he gathered his thoughts, "I was up to my neck in that operation. When he took that coke it caused a real stink for the firm and a major embarrassment for me. Loughlin's the loose end of that story and that will have to be tied up."

"We'll have to use a 'K' to take him out." said Dixon.
"A 'K', yes a 'K', someone we can deny if he's caught, not a member of the firm, a 'K'." Simpson took a sip of his coffee.

"I've already checked who's available," said Dixon, "and we've got a man in place already."
"Clever girl, I've taught you well." Simpson gave Dixon a nod of approval.

"His name is Gorman and he's in Longmoore already."
"Gorman? That name rings a bell, give me his brief."
"He's ex-SAS, served all over the world, but got badly wounded and was pensioned off."
"Carry on," said Simpson.

"After leaving the regiment he came to work for us as a 'K' on deniable ops, but he was caught by his partner using heroin in Afghanistan while teaching the Mujahidin how to use Stinger surface-to-air missiles against the Russian helicopters. The firm abandoned him there to fend for himself, he was lucky to get out of Afghanistan with his life. When he got back to England he still had the drug habit but no money, hence Longmoore."

"Drugs?" said Simpson.
"He's been clean now for years." replied Dixon.
"I remember him now," said Simpson, "he's Irish also," Simpson was now smiling as a new plan was unfolding in his head, "and he knows me well, I'll handle this myself."

Saturday 11 am

Pat finished shaving and walked the corridor to Conor's room. They're called rooms in D-cat, not cells.

"What d'ya think Conor? Sunday best?" Pat stood in his best clothes, a pair of Nike trainers with blue Levi 501's, a blue Ralph Lauren shirt, a black Rockport bomber jacket and belt.

"Where you goin'," said Conor.
"I got word about my first town visit."
"What!" Conor sat up in his bed
"I'm gettin' picked up at twelve o'clock by a man I used to work for, maybe he's going to offer me a job when I get out.
"Fuck off Pat, you were a Brit. You never worked."

The term 'Brit' being synonymous with soldier in Belfast, after all the British soldiers on the street during the troubles.

"I worked for security when I got out."

"You liar!" Conor shouted as if there was some law against telling lies in jail.

"Fuck off jealous arse; I'll see you when I get back." Pat lifted Conor's trainers, ran up the corridor and threw them in the showers.
"Bastard!" Conor shouted then lay down again happy for Pat

The ride in Simpson's Range Rover made Pat feel like a man again. It had been years since he had even rode in a car, let alone sat up front, the last car he had been in was a police car at his arrest. Since then he was always handcuffed in the back of a van that looked like a horse-box. The Range Rover was beautiful, dark navy with cream leather, a man's car.

"So Pat, it's great to see you after all these years." Simpson was as patronising as he ever was.
"I take it this is not a social visit," said Pat as he gazed out of the window and savoured his freedom.
"No Pat, it's not. There's work for you if you want it." Simpson turned into a pub car park just fifteen minutes from the prison; "We'll talk over lunch." he carried on.

The pub was a large country style establishment with a fake thatched roof. Inside was dimly lit with big wooden benches in the middle, and semi-circular booths with smaller tables and softer seating. The walls had the theme of the countryside with horse belts and an old plough hung from the wooden beams in the ceiling. A market cart stood in the corner being used as a salad bar, an 'Eat As Much As You Like' sign hung above it.

The pub was a popular eating-house and was used by the business type as well as the young and trendy who flocked there for the cheap cocktails. Pat and Simpson took the corner booth.

Simpson spoke as they ate. Pat had an eight-ounce sirloin steak with chips and fried onion rings: Simpson had a club sandwich.

"Pat we have a problem. A stone in our shoe that you can remove."
"How much money?" Pat cut straight to the chase.
"Same as usual, you'll be on £300 a day."
"Do you have my documents, am I leaving right away?"
"No Pat, you're not leaving anywhere just yet, it's in the prison."
"What!" Pat had a look of shock on his face.
"Let me explain."

Simpson told the story about how in 1994 the SIS had been financing the loyalist terrorists in Belfast to fight the IRA. The firm could not be seen to be giving the loyalists guns that were British or American made so they supplied them with cocaine that they could use as a currency to acquire AK47 assault rifles from the Russian Mafia. The Russians wanted the coke and the deal was done. The IPLO hijacked the consignment and it was never seen again because the IRA executed all the principal player's except for one and he was now in Longmoore, Conor Loughlin.

"We're sure Loughlin knows where the cocaine is and may try to retrieve it now that the peace process is under way. He may think that it is safe for him to go back into Belfast."

"How much coke?" said Pat.

"If it hit the street it's worth millions and that can't happen." Simpson got more serious, "More than that Pat, the cocaine ties us to the loyalists and we can't be seen to have our name and drugs mentioned in the same sentence, do you understand?"

Pat paused for a few moments; his brain went into overdrive. 'Conor,' he thought, 'One of those bastards, but he's my friend. Fuck it; this was how it had to be.' This was what he had been trained to do from a boy soldier at seventeen. Conor would just have to be another statistic. This was Pat's way out of jail, back into 'The Firm' and his life back. Pat nodded his head.

Simpson handed Pat a package he had taken from his briefcase. "You'll have to check that in the toilet."

"I hope there's money in there," said Pat.

"There's £1000 in cash to get you started and a passport and driving licence for when we pick you up. There'll be three hundred deposited onto those credit cards after that for each day that you work."

"Weapon." said Pat, "Shall I use my initiative?"

"No Pat. It's got to be high profile. In that package you will find a Ruger SP101 .38 special and five wad cutter rounds."

"Wads? That's a bit excessive, they'd drop an elephant."

"Listen Pat, it has to be like this. That's the weapon the IRA used to kill Paul O'Neill in one of their drinking dens. It was recovered during a search in Ballymurphy in 1996

and we've been keeping it for an occasion such as this. Loughlin has to die with the same weapon as his boss, and then the IRA will get the blame."
"Reasonable." said Pat.

"There's more Pat." Simpson put his hand on Pat's arm to keep him seated. "Julie Murphy, Loughlin is having an affair with her."
"Long time ago, I know all about it." Pat was going into work mode.
"No Pat. We can't be sure what she knows. When Loughlin gets it she might run to the press. She'll have to be eliminated also."
"Unless they're in the same room, so it looks as if she's caught in crossfire, it won't work. The IRA wouldn't do a senseless murder." Pat had spent too many years fighting the IRA; he knew how they worked.

"It will have to be done at her flat." Simpson let go of his arm. "In there you'll also find a vial that contains some semen and two pubic hairs. They belong to a known child-rapist and killer who has been too smart to convict. Police took the hairs as part of a DNA sample; we found the semen after putting a trigger (surveillance) on his house and sifting through his rubbish for six months. It was in a used condom in his bin."

Pat took a look into the package.
"Not in public Pat," Simpson put his hand on the bag, "make it look like a rape. Get into her flat and strangle her and spread the contents of that vial on her genitals. We'll kill two birds with one stone. We'll lift you afterwards."

"OK let me get into character." Pat lifted the package and went into the toilet.

Pat locked the cubicle door behind him and opened the package. The gun was a nickel-plated snub nose revolver with a rubber handle. He checked the serial numbers; they had been drilled off. He opened the weapon and checked the chamber. Empty. Firing pin. Sound. Then he took five flat nose bullets and put them in the chambers.

The SP101 is unlike most revolvers. Most hold six; this holds five. That's not many compared to most semi-automatic pistols that can hold up to seventeen. The SP101 is meant for close up work and with wad cutter rounds, if you need more than one, then you shouldn't be in that kind of work.

As Pat checked the rest of the contents he was thinking of all that Simpson had said: 'Conor and the IPLO, millions of pounds worth of cocaine, the IRA and Julie Murphy.' A shiver ran up Pat's back and a bead of sweat ran down his neck as the truth hit home. 'I'm in a no-win situation here,' he thought. 'That's why I've been told the whole story. A 'K' is usually kept in the dark. You get your brief, do your job and try to get out safe. It's no concern to a 'K' what he's being paid for, and he doesn't care. I know too much now. An IRA weapon in the hands of an Irish man in an English jail; there's no way will I walk out of there; look how they treated me in Afghanistan. And Julie Murphy is that only a bluff to make me think that I'm in the firm again. Will I be dropped at the prison gate or will I get it at the pick up point when Julie's dead so they can stitch that nonce up?'

Pat put his documents into the inside of his bomber jacket, checked the weapon to make sure the firing pin would strike the percussion cap of the bullet and tucked the weapon into the waist band of his jeans, at the front left hand side just under his jacket, which he fastened with the metal push button for easy access in case a quick draw was needed. His jacket was long enough to conceal it.

Simpson smiled and lifted his briefcase as he stood up. Then sat down quicker than he had ever done in his past life; as a spray of thick red blood and grey matter changed the colour of the blonde bimbo's hair, who was sitting behind him, and turned her pinacolada into a bloody Mary. The horse belts and brass bed warmers on the wall got a fresh coat of crimson as the second round hit Simpson in the forehead. There was a trickle of blood from the small entry wounds on his forehead that at first glance would have looked like minor wounds. But the mess of blood, skull and brain that were pouring from the cavity exit wounds and giving the walls a makeover told the whole story.

People dived for cover as Pat took Simpson's wallet from his firm's suit. 'It will take them hours to find out who he is,' Pat thought to himself as he looked at Simpson's ID and took the keys for the Range Rover. Pat smashed the vial of semen as he drove back to pick-up Conor.

10

Julie saw Pat walk very briskly across the car park as she packed-up her belongings into the boot of her Ford Escort. 'I wonder what's up with him,' she thought, 'I don't care, I'm out of here,' then she walked back in to the prison to collect more of her stuff.

"Right Conor on your feet we're going!" Pat barked an order as Conor lay watching a fight on Saturday sport.
"Goin'? You're fucking right I'm goin' ya big mouthed bastard ye." Conor snapped back.
"What a ya bleedin' on aboot, come on we're fuckin off now"
"Julie just called to see me," said Conor, "and she told me they know everything. She's left and I'm getting shipped out on Monday. Who'd ya tell Pat?"
"I told no one, come on we've got to go Conor."
"Nah you're a wanker Pat."
"Conor, we've got to go."

Pat briefly told Conor of the days events and Conor put his wet trainers on.
"Conor, you and her are in grave danger."
"No shit Sherlock. Let's catch her before she goes." Conor was really concerned for Julie.

"Fuck her, let's go Conor."
"No Pat, I LOVE HER!"

Pat and Conor walked towards Julie's office trying to look and act their normal casual selves but the expression on their faces told another story.

"I hope she's still here," said Conor.
"Don't matter. I know where she lives." Pat didn't even look at Conor as he replied.
"What! Pat!"
"It's alright Conor, we're altogether now. Tell me about the coke, is it still there?"
"Certainly it is; Taffy even has a man to buy the lot for a mill."
"That's sound" said Pat "cuz we're gonna need it to disappear, big time."
Conor grabbed the handle and they burst into Julie's office without knocking.

"No need for formalities Julie, we're in a hurry. Who'd you tell?"
"What?" said Julie as she packed her last book into a cardboard box.
"About you an him," he pointed at Conor.
"You didn't," she looked at Conor and he dropped his head.
"Not everything and he's my best mate."
"Conor," she put her hand on his chin and lifted his face to look at him.

"Right there's no time for a lovers tiff," said Pat, "I'll tell you how it is."

"Pat very briefly told again some of the day's events.

"You don't seem to realise the severity of this Julie," Pat carried on, *"who did you tell?"*
"Only my twin sister and she wouldn't have said a word to anyone."
"Is that right? Get on that phone." Pat handed Julie the receiver.
"Dominic!" said Julie. Pat was already moving towards the door before Julie hung up.

"That fuckin' poof let the secret out. He caused all this trouble." Pat stopped and turned. "We've got about 6 hours before the police lift that body and get it finger printed, then all hell is gonna break loose. Right you two." Pat was in control now and both Conor and Julie knew it.

"You Conor, you find Taffy and get a phone number and get a meet on for two weeks then help Julie with that box. There are no cameras here so you'll be able to lie down in the back of her car. I'll see you at Julie's in an hour."
"What!" said Julie.
"Don't fuck about now Julie," said Pat, "I'm trying to save all our lives."

Conor put his arm around Julie's shoulder and she put hers around his waist.
"I'm away to fix Dominic's wagon for him," Pat said as he left the room.
"What does he mean by that?" asked Julie.
"Never mind." Conor smiled, "let's go."

They pecked a kiss on each other's lips. Conor lifted the box and they walked through the door. Julie stopped to look back.

"Let's go babe." Julie shut the door.

***

Dominic smiled at Pat as he towel dried his legs, holding the top part of his towel to hide his modesty. Pat smiled back as he pulled off his shirt and started to undo his trainers, never taking his eyes of Dominic. Dominic's eyes lit up as Pat gave him a wink and carried on undressing, Dominic dropped the towel as Pat nodded towards the shower. Dominic turned and walked back towards the shower again naked. When he turned the corner, Pat pulled his trainers back on and then followed him.

Dominic was still smiling when he heard Pat's footsteps, but his face turned into a frown when he saw that Pat was still half-clothed. Pat stepped closer and hit Dominic with his open palm, trying to catch him with the heel of his hand and drive his nose up into his brain, but the steam and the wet floor made Dominic slip at impact and he caught Pat's thumb in his mouth. He bit down hard.

The pain was like an electric shock going up Pat's arm. Dominic fell to his knees, still biting down hard on Pat's thumb. He could feel his mouth fill up with blood. Pat tried to pull his hand away but it made Dominic bite down even harder. He wrapped his arms around Pat's chest in a bear hug and squeezed tight as he rose to his feet. Pat's eyes felt as though they would pop out as it was getting hard to breathe. He tried to wrap his legs around Dominic's waist, to give himself some leverage to fight back, but Dominic was a big lad and he had to struggle to interlock his feet. As soon as he did he squeezed as hard as he could and got his other thumb and rammed it into Dominic's eye. Dominic let out a high-pitched squeal as a thick dollop of claret squirted out onto Pat's face and Dominic's eye popped out onto his cheekbone. Pat now had two free hands and grabbed Dominic by the back of his hair, just where his highlights were growing out and pulled his head back exposing his chin. Pat then rammed his other hand under Dominic's chin and at the same time lifted his head and turned it, stretching his neck. Pat could see the terror in Dominic's good eye as he knew what was coming next. Dominic's neck broke at the axis-joint at the base of the skull. Pat kept on twisting his head, like he was opening a bottle of champagne, Dominic's legs gave way and they fell to the floor.

11

The Stenna HSS is the largest catamaran that ferries from Holyhead in Wales to Dun Laoghaire, 20 miles south of Dublin. It's at least the size of a football pitch and has three floors on which to park your vehicle. With its massive size it carries articulated lorries as well as cars, motorcycles and caravans for the holidaymakers who may be on a fishing or golfing trip to Ireland; it also has walk-on passengers. This is how Conor, Pat and Julie chose to travel.

The tickets were bought separately, in case anybody was looking out for three people travelling together, Pat hung back and watched Conor and Julie board first. The security, who Pat knew were really special branch, didn't even look twice at the happy couple who looked like newlyweds as they kissed before letting go of each others hands, and then passed through the kind of metal detector that is usually found in airports. Pat knew he was right to have left the Ruger .38 behind. In fact, it was now in the biggest armoury in Britain: the river Thames.

Simpson's Range Rover had been parked up in a hotel car park in Holyhead, where it wouldn't be found for days.

Pat followed the herd from the departure lounge, up the boarding ramp and onto the ferry. He navigated his way through a crowd of screaming children and teenagers who were jockeying for position to get the best machine in the video arcade, or trying to be first in the queue for the on-board McDonalds.

He caught sight of Conor, who was doing his best impersonation of a stork, as he propped up the bar and took a sip from that long, cold Budweiser that he had thought so long about. 'He looks like he's kissing Julie,' Pat thought as he approached.

The two televisions above Conor's head, and set back into the surrounding of the bar, had American sports playing. An American football with baseball bat and glove adorned the walls. A neon sign reading *Strikers' Sports Bar* gave off an ambient glow, and a croupier stood to Conor's left with a deck of cards playing Blackjack.

"Julie's at the toilet," Conor handed Pat a bottle of Bud and stirred a Southern Comfort with lemonade that Pat presumed was for Julie.
"Sound Conor, we've a bit to talk about before she comes back."

The captain gave some announcement about the crossing and the video screens changed to show some safety procedures about how to put a life jacket on.

"You'd probably freeze to death out there," said Conor. All Pat cared about was the crossing time.

"Ninety minutes," said the captain.

"Conor, both of you know the full story now, but I'm sure Julie's really freaked out. When I leave you at the other side make sure you emphasise the fact that all this was done to save *all* our lives, make sure you keep her calm, assure her that all will be okay." Pat wasn't so sure himself that it would be, but he had to keep his troop's morale together.

"What do you mean 'leave us' Pat? We're going to Belfast together."

"I'm not leaving you for good, dick head; we have no weapons with us. I'm an ex-Brit, for fucks sake. The 'Ra' would still stiff me, and we have to go onto the Falls Road to get the coke..."

"I suppose you're right," Conor interrupted, "where you gonna get a gun?"

"Look it would be better if you and Julie get the train to Belfast and book into the Europa Hotel as newlyweds and I will call you when I get there. I still have a few friends in Ballymun. I can pick up a weapon there."

"Get me one too Pat." Conor spoke excitedly.

"You just look after her and make sure the charlie is okay, I'll do the rest."

Julie waved and bounced up the corridor smiling. Her long loose black curls danced about her shoulders, one was stuck to her neck where it had got wet at the sink. She wore a three-quarters length black leather coat with a fur collar that came down to her waist in a V and could be buttoned and tied with a belt, that hung to the sides as she wore the coat open. Matching black ankle boots and belt, with blue jeans that sat so well over her hips Armani should have been paying her to wear them. A tight blue T-shirt showed-off a figure that her work clothes so purposefully hid.

"Hi guys," she kissed Conor on the cheek as he handed her the Southern Comfort and lemonade.
"You look very beautiful," said Pat.
"Thank you," Julie smiled.
'Now there's a change of heart,' thought Conor, he liked them all being friends.

The boat gave a judder and vibrated as the two giant, turbine engines were started. The captain explained what was happening and that it would only be a few minutes before they were underway.

Conor and Pat gave a look of relief to each other as the craft slowly pulled away from the dock, clearing the harbour walls and heading out to sea.

"So Conor, tell me about this Mary McAuley; how you know her and stuff, just so I can get a bit of a picture in my head as to what we're dealing with."
"Fuck all Pat, there's nothing really to say, she's only a wee girl."

Conor gestured, not wanting to talk about past girlfriends in front of Julie, but Pat didn't care.

"You must have known a bit about her to leave the stuff in her flat?" asked Pat. A couple of children stumbled and spilt some pop on Julie's jeans, as the seas got heavier. Julie used this as an excuse to let the boys talk.

"I'll go and clean this up at the toilets."

"We'll be sitting over there," Conor pointed to a cubicle, free from any marauding children.

"Okay," said Julie, "can you get me a club sandwich?" The boys called a waitress as they took their seats.

"Well Pat," said Conor, "Mary's from Newry herself. We first met when we were fourteen; I was best friends with her brother Joe; we were always trying to get a few quid. Now my Ma, she got a new set of blankets for the house. There were no duvets in Newry in those days; new blankets were like gold dust. They were wrapped up in that hard, see-through plastic that you sometimes see on the seats of taxies."

"Aye, I know the sort." Pat was smiling as he thought about the old days back in Dublin.

"Go on."

"Well my Ma, she was showing them to everyone, the priest, the milkman, Curly, Larry and Mo for God's sake, everybody wanted to see Sadie's new blankets. She had them for a month and wouldn't open them, so me and Joe came up with a cunning plan." Conor's eyes lit up with devilment as he took a sip of his Bud. Pat was enjoying the story.

"There was this mobile shop-van at the corner of our street, well; it wasn't really mobile, coz it was up on breeze-blocks: the fucking thing didn't go anywhere, but it was a big blue Bedford van anyway."
"Go on," Pat was having a good craic.

"Anyway, this van had a big roll of cloakroom tickets on one of the shelves. I don't know what the fuck they had them there for, but they sat there for years. Well, when I was chatting up the wee girl that worked there, Joe stole the tickets and fucked off."
"Then what did you do?"

"Well, we lived in Drumalane, a real shit-hole council-estate, but at the top of the hill, there was a new private estate called Ardaveen. Most of the houses were bought by people from our estate, who had got jobs at the new Norbrooke chemical factory, so we just thought that they were a better class of hooligan."
"Your mad, ya boy ye," laughed Pat.

"So I threw the blankets out of our bedroom window, Joe caught them and off we went to Ardaveen to sell a raffle for the adventure playground football team. Swear to fuck Pat, they were nearly fighting with each other to buy the tickets. We told them that the draw would be at the community centre, the following Saturday. We'd planned to hide down by the canal and watch them all fighting and arguing over the missing blankets; it would have been funny as fuck.

"Now, we were walking down the road happy as pigs in shit, with four pockets full of 10p's and 50p's, and there's Mary and Sally Young standing on the corner and seen us with all the kit. 'I'm telling my mammy on you,' she shouts as her and Sally ran home. We had too much change in our pockets, and two big parcels of blankets to catch them, so when we turned a corner our two mas' were standing at the door. His ma had a belt, and mine had a wooden Scholl shoe and we got the shit beat out of us and our money took off us. The two auld bastards kept all the money too." Conor gave a sly laugh.

"So Mary touted on you to your ma, you dickhead." Pat was having a good laugh. "It was a good plan though Conor."
"I know, I met her at a disco about a year later and we had a good laugh about it, we even became boyfriend and girlfriend. Pat, I was with her till we were seventeen, we even lost our virginity together. Now that was a carry-on. We were seventeen and none of the two of us knew what to do, it took two days to get it right and then it only lasted 1 minute. 'Fuckin' mad.' Once sex raised its ugly head, that was me away Pat, shagging everything that moved. When I came into the house the fish stopped swimming."
"You're fuckin' mad Conor."

"Mary got pissed off and fucked off to Belfast; and after my cousin got killed, I got in touch with her and went to Belfast also. She was working for the IPLO as a prostitute, and that's how I got involved with them."
"I wouldn't think you'd find her too hard to talk to then Conor," said Pat. "Here comes Julie."

"No, told ya, all will be sound."

The boat docked on time, Julie and Conor left first and they stopped at the Irish special branch. An officer in a green, reflective jacket asked: 'Irish or English?' There's no passport check between England and Ireland, the police are more concerned about illegal immigrants from eastern-Europe and are happy just to hear your accent.

"Oh were Irish," Julie came back in her American accent. The guard didn't even blink as he had heard thousands of American tourists profess their Irishness every year. And she wasn't lying anyway; her father was from Cork. The guard waved them through and thought to himself, 'If your great-grandfather owned an Irish Wolf-hound or a Kerry-blue terrier, you'd get yourself an Irish passport.' Pat just walked through with, "Cad é mar á tá tú" (how are you doing, in Irish). They all knew the plan: Conor and Julie went to get the train to Belfast; Pat went to Ballymun. Pat thought all this went too easily, 'I won't let my guard slip.'

***

"The rumours that are going about the jail are mad," said Taffy, as he dipped his chocolate biscuits into a cup-a-soup.
"Yeah what went on?" Spooner screwed up his face as he watched Taffy lick the hot chocolate and soup.

"I'm not too sure, but we've been locked down for two days. That queer who killed the kid was found by the gym-screw, with his head turned round like that kid from the exorcist."

"How the fuck did that happen?" asked Spooner.

"I don't know what's going on, but they say he slipped in the shower; one of those freak accidents, like a million-to-one chance."

"Fuckin mad innit!"

"Yeah," said Gary, "Conor's mate Pat fucked off that day also. People are saying he had something to do with it, as he was the gym orderly."

"What do you think Gary?"

"No way, he's just a mad paddy. Nice lad though; but fucking mad. Anyway, he was on a town-visit that day, and never came back."

"Do you think he's in on this thing with Conor?" Spooner was gathering all the facts. He smiled, laughed and made gestures of joking that, to on-lookers in the visiting area, it would look like a visit between friends and not the sinister plot that was being drawn-up.

"Probably, that's why I think Conor done one as well. Does it matter?"

"No," said Spooner, "he's just another one who'll get the 'good news' if he needs it when we take the coke off them. In fact it might be better; Conor will feel more confident with his mate with him."

"Yeah, your right." Gary was nodding his head and smiling.

"Yeah their arses will open when the boys pop up with a couple of nine-millimetres."

"So listen Spooner, I'm going to come out tomorrow and wait on the car, I've only a couple more months to do, but knowing I've got some serious 'dough' waiting for me, the twenty days extra will be fuck all."

The two screws took no notice as the plot thickened.

"Did you hear about that killing in the pub up the road from here?" asked Gary.
"It's all very hush-hush, but the word on the street is that it's Russian Mafia or CIA. He was some big noise in the military intelligence. I've heard every rumour, IRA, INLA, CIA, SAS, PLO, MI5, It's fucking like alphabet soup."
"Mad innit," said Gary.
"I'll tell you what," Spooner carried on, "whoever did do it knew what the fuck they were at; a real professional job."
"You don't want to be messing around with that firm," said Gary.
"No fucking way mate, they can keep all that shit."

***

"Thirty Euros, one way! What kind of money is that?" Conor looked at the change in his hand as Julie kicked off her boots and played footsie in the first-class carriage of the Dublin to Belfast train.

The woman in the green uniform with the little hat that any Thunderbirds fan would be proud of, took Conor's Stirling and paid him in a mixture of Euro coins and English Pounds.

"Fifty four pounds each, that was alrigh," said Conor, "but she could have given us all Stirling since we are going north."

"She gave you mostly Stirling Conor, that big one's a two-pound coin"

"Two-pound coin!" said Conor, "it looks just like the Euros."

"I think that's the whole point Conor, the government are getting us all used to the coin so it wont be such a culture shock when the change-over eventually happens. It's going to happen anyway so they should just get on with it."

"Did you ever see an Irish two-pound coin Julie?"

"I've never seen any Irish money Conor."

"Two, one-pound coins cello-taped together." Conor started laughing and finished off his bottle of Bud, Julie just shook her head.

The journey from Dublin to Belfast takes about two hours and the scenery is breathtaking.

Out of the city of Dublin, which itself is very beautiful, not having been bombed during the wars; as the Irish Republic was neutral. It still has its Victorian architecture and sprawling parklands. Then out towards Skerries, Mosney and the seaside. The train then comes back in country through parkland and forest.

After an hour, Drogheda, where Conor told the story of how in 1690, King James of England fought King William of Holland (William of Orange) and used Irish troops to fight their battle on Irish soil at the Boyne River, Drogheda. Catholic troops verses Protestant troops.

"And that's what most of the trouble is about today."
"The Irish have long memories," said Julie.
"Well it's not the whole story, but it's a good enough start for ya."

The train stopped at Newry and Conor was able to point-out his hometown, where he had played as a child and the old landmarks pulled at his heartstrings.
"You will have to bring me here Conor, and let me see your hometown."
"No Julie, there's nothing left for us here anymore."

As the train pulled off Julie asked, "What's that on the top of the hill?"
"That's the last of the army observation posts; they can look into the Republic and into the North. There used to be a massive checkpoint there also, at the border. The IRA were forever attacking them when we were kids, but that's all stopped now, with the peace process." Conor carried on and Julie was impressed with his knowledge of history.

"You know this place has so much culture Julie." Conor spoke and got goose bumps as he told the story of Cuchulian. "You see the observation post? Well at the time of the Celts Ireland was like; four countries: Ulster, Munster, Linster and Connaught, each had its own king, and the whole country had a high-king who sat at Tara, in the middle of Ireland.

Ulster's king was King Conor and they had a champion called Cuchulian, who fought the Connaught army, which was led by the warrior queen, Maeve. He fought them single-handedly and swooped down from that hill where the observation post stands, and fought them at the ford; and all over a bull. It's all mythology, but it makes great stories."
"Stop there," said Julie, "I'll get us another drink."

Conor watched Julie approach and thought how lucky he was. The train took a slight bend in the track and rattled over a loose sleeper which made Julie stumble, her Southern and lemonade splashed a couple who, if they were not gay, were doing a great impersonation of the Village People. One had a crew cut and cap-sleeve T-shirt; the other had a moustache that any Hells Angel would have been proud of. Crew Cut steadied her up and moustache just smiled.

"Are you alright?" said Conor, as she sat the drinks on the table. "Lucky YMCA was there to catch you."
"I'm sure I've seen him somewhere before," said Julie as she sat down facing Conor, "maybe on the boat."
"Nah, ya wouldn't forget that face," said Conor. The Village People didn't even look at them as the train pulled into Belfast Central Station.

12

A hand grabbed Conor by the collar and dragged him into the hallway. Mary popped her head out and looked up and down the dimly lit balcony to make sure that no one was watching, then locked and bolted the door.

"Jesus Christ! Conor Loughlin! What are you doing here?" Conor just smiled and put his arms out to receive her.

Mary reached up and around Conor's neck and planted a kiss full on his mouth. Not deep and wet and passionate, like lovers, but with the emotion of long lost friends and of secrets between past lovers.

"Conor, the IRA would kill you if they knew you were here."
"Fuck them! I'm hardly going to tell them am I?"
"What are you doing here; do you want a cup of tea?"
Mary was in a tizzy as she walked towards the kitchen.
"I just got out of jail in England and wanted to see you coz I was in Belfast; milk no sugar Mary."

Mary handed Conor a mug and led him into the living room.

"Gees Mary! You've still got your figure after all these years."

"Cheeky git!" said Mary, "I'm not twenty-eight yet!"

Mary looked after herself, she was tall and slim and her heart shaped ass was kept that way through daily visits to the gym. She kept her hair straight and bleached blonde, but she wore a little too much gold.

"So what's been going on in your life then Loughlin?"

"Told ya; I was in jail in England." They entered the living room and Conor took a breath. "You've done well for yourself Mary."

He sat down gingerly on the green leather settee, the wooden floor had a green Persian rug on it and a wide-screen TV with matching DVD and Hi-fi, which stood in the corner. A large yew-wood dining table and chairs with matching green upholstery could be seen though the archway into the dining area.

"Yeah, I keep the place nice Conor, but I'm still on the Falls Road."

"You must be getting a few quid Mary, why don't you move away?"

"I will when I've finished Conor, but this is where the money is, I have 20 girls working for me, and I have to look after my interests besides," she carried on, "the police still don't come around here very much, so it's pretty safe to work."

"Yeah," said Conor, "I suppose the IRA get their arm into ye?"
"I've a business partner; he takes care of all that."
"Who's that then?" said Conor.
"You don't know him," Mary winked at Conor.

The next hour or so was spent catching up on old times and reminiscing about Newry. Conor looked fondly on Mary but wanted to go back to the hotel, and Julie.

"Are you staying the night then Conor?" Mary hoped.
"Nah Mary, I've someone waiting for me in the Europa; but will you come down tomorrow night for a drink?"
"No problem Conor, I'll get ready and drive you down there; don't want anybody seeing ya boy."
Conor followed Mary up the stairs of the maisonette.
"Where you going?" she said as she turned the corner to the bathroom.
"Can I just look around for old time sake, Mary?"
"Course ya can love, I'll see you down stairs."

Mary's bedroom had changed so much since Conor had last been there. A brass four-poster bed played centre stage, white mesh nets hung invitingly from the post and fondled the duvet and scattered pillows. The light from the amber streetlight smiled at Conor as he touched the bedclothes.

The walls had black and white prints, the one above the headboard showed a semi-naked couple kissing, the man behind her kissing her as she looked up at him and dripped some cologne on her breasts, 'tasteful,' Conor thought, as he ran his fingers over the duvet.

The window had wooden slat, vertical blinds with a brass curtain rail that held two sets of curtains. A green set of drapes at each end of the pole that hung straight and a cream and green Egyptian pattern, that hung in a sweep from the middle, to brass tie-backs and on down to the corner of the room. This is where Conor knelt, pulling back the carpet.

The carpet was new and still had the smell of rubber and Hessian and everything virginal that tempts your senses in an expensive furniture shop.

The floorboards were untreated, tongue-and-groove and the corner-board was held in place by two panel-pins, that Conor found easy to remove with his Leatherman, pocket tool, which he had found in the glove-box of the range rover and acquired for himself.

He used the blade to prise the board from its bed; he then sat it down on the underside of the flipped-over carpet to keep it in place so he could look into the hole.

The dust made him sneeze as he lifted out the first packet. It was a square block, about six inches, by four, by one, covered in thick plastic that looked as though it had been vac-packed. The package had been re-sealed with a strip of black insulation tape. Conor remembered the packages and thought of Sean O'Rourke's words: 'I'll take a whack out of it for me, you and McGuire; fuck sake, you can even give Mary some.'

"Come on Conor, are you ready to go?" Mary shouted up the stairs and brought Conor back to the real world again.

"Two minutes love." He looked into the hole and saw all the cocaine. His fortune smiled back at him.

"I'm coming now!" He replaced the floorboard then slipped the kilo of cocaine into his jacket and walked to the top of the stairs; he was still smiling as they got into the car.

13

Ballymun is one of the most run-down areas in Ireland and is in stark contrast to the beauty of Dublin City Centre. It has large tenement flats and grass-ways that when first constructed in the1960's were meant for children to play on. Now all that plays are the hordes that gather around the burnt-out cars; or the few horses and ponies that the children keep as pets. There are running battles with the police and animal welfare, who try to round up the horses. On occasion, horses have been found some twenty-odd floors up inside the flats. The area is rife with drugs, prostitution and guns, in-fact Ballymun makes most of the ghettos in Western Europe, or the USA for that matter, look like Beverly Hills. Pat was sitting in the penthouse.

"Well Pat," said Ginty, a short fat man about 5' 6" with dark hair and complexion. He was about forty five years old and wore a designer track suit that looked ridiculous on a body that the last time had seen the inside of a gym was at roll-call at one of the few times it had been at school. Four fat, heavy gold chains hung at different levels around his neck and each finger threatened with a gold sovereign ring or nugget that Huggie Bear would have been well proud of, straight from 'Pimps R Us'.

Ginty might have looked as if he spent most of his day with his face buried in a bargain bucket of Kentucky Fried Chicken, which he probably did, but he was no slouch when he came to making money. Everything and anything that was going down in Ballymun, or Dublin for that matter, Ginty had his fat little hand in it.

"Let me get this right, you're away from Dublin twenty bleedin' years, running with the fuckin British army and all of a sudden you're back, lookin' to borrow a fuckin' gun. I'll tell you what; you've balls like a stallion."

"Now Ginty, we go back a long way." Pat wasn't flapping at all as he watched Ginty bawl and pace the floor, waving his arms and pointing his fingers. He could care less for the ruthless reputation Ginty had built for himself as a killer. Pat knew him from old, besides none of the 'Ginty Gang' was here. There was just Ginty and a twenty-five-year-old woman who sat smoking what Pat thought was hashish, but the little brown rocks were crack cocaine.

"Anyway, I have a job to do up-north," said Pat, "and if all goes well I'll bring you back some coke; an ounce for yourself, and as much as you want to buy."
"What!" said Ginty, "now you're talkin' my game."
"Well sit down before you have a heart-attack, ya bleedin' eejit."
"Bunny, give me good friend Pat a smoke of that."
"No, you're all right," said Pat, "I've work to do." Bunny didn't even take her lips of the pipe.

"Bunny go and get a couple of beers from the fridge, me and Pat have to do a bit of talkin'."

Bunny stood up and her white, silk dressing gown opened and showed she wore nothing underneath. Her long, red locks covered her breasts and Pat felt a stirring in his loins as she was the first naked woman he had seen in years.

"Ooops!" she giggled as she walked to the kitchen.
"She yours?" asked Pat.
"Anybody's." laughed Ginty.
"Why do you call her Bunny?"
"Cuz she fucks like a rabbit."
"I heard that." Bunny giggled in the kitchen.

"So what's happening up-north then?" Ginty sat on the edge of his seat.
"I can't tell you. It'll take a couple of days, but it's sound. I just have to stand-off and make sure nobody fucks around when the stuff is lifted."

"I've just the tool for ya," said Ginty as he rose to his feet. "Bunny, look after Pat there, I'll not be long." He winked at Pat as he left.

Bunny came back from the kitchen with a couple of bottles of beer in one hand and the crack pipe in the other.

"There you go." she handed Pat the beers. The first bottle he drank in one go, never taking his eyes off Bunny, who was now sitting facing him on the edge of the chair, her eyes closed as she took a double helping of crack. Her legs parted slightly as she fell back in the chair, holding her breath for as long as possible. Pat nearly swallowed the other bottle as he looked between her legs.

"Do you wanna fuck?" Bunny said as she rose to her feet and dropped her silk gown. She walked to the side of the settee where she bent over and put her hands on the arm of the chair.
"Come on then." She wiggled her ass.
"Oh fuck you're beautiful!" said Pat, and she was.

"I've three rules you can't break," she said as Pat dropped his trousers. "One, don't kiss me."
'No chance!' thought Pat.
"Two, don't touch the back of my neck."
"OK."
"Three; and this is the most important one, don't touch my hair."
"OK, OK." Pat was ready to burst.
"Well spit on it and get going while I still love ya with this shit in me big lad."
She giggled and gave her ass another little wiggle.

Bunny's skin felt as soft and smooth as her silk gown. She pushed back onto him. Warm. Wet. Soft. Deep. Five years of badness was trying to get out of Pat. He ran his hands over her and cupped her small, pert breasts.

"Fuck me!" She pushed hard onto him. "Fuck me, fuck me." He squeezed her nipples. Pat's excitement grew and he bent forward squeezing her waist tight with his arms.

"Fuck me!" She screamed. Pat ran his hands over her back, as his excitement grew stronger.

"I told you not to touch the back of my neck man." She stopped moving.

"Sorry, sorry." Pat tried to compose himself. It was no use, wild horses couldn't stop him, he was in a frenzy, and his hand became entangled in her hair.

"Leave my hair alone!" She screamed as Pat lost control and played her like a yo-yo.

"Stop your fuckin' moaning!" said Pat, "you'd think I was fuckin' married to ya!"

"I told you not to touch my hair!" She screamed louder as she stuck a little two-inch penknife, that Ginty had been using as a letter-opener, into Pat's thigh. He didn't feel the pain at first as other things were happening down below, but his right hand soon joined the other at the back of her head at high-impact as he saw the knife in his leg.

"You fuckin' bitch!" he shouted as she fell to the ground.

"What the fuck are you doing hitting my girl?" Ginty was standing in the doorway, unfolding the stock and putting the magazine into the parachute-regiment-version of the Kalashnikov AKM assault rifle.

14

The Europa hotel in Belfast stands in Great Victoria Street. To the rear of the hotel there is a coach station next to the hotel's nightclub, 'Paradise Lost'. The hotel has a shopping arcade at one side and an open street at the other side of the building with Belfast Grand Opera House taking the other corner. Facing the hotel are two of Belfast's most well-known drinking establishments; Robinson's Bar and The Crown Liquor Salon, the latter being owned by the National Trust as it is one of, if not the oldest pub in Ireland and has been featured in movies as far back as the1940's. This is where the 'Village People' sat and watched Mary drop-off Conor.

"You go follow her back," said Crew Cut, "and I'll keep a trigger on the hotel until you come back."

Moustache lifted the keys for the Vauxhall Astra they had hired from Avis Rent a Car, just up the road from the Europa.

"Get a 'P check' (personnel check) on the number plate." Moustache scribbled down Mary's registration number and gave it to Crew Cut.

"If it matches where she parks-up, we're cooking with gas mate."

Mary gave Conor a little kiss goodbye and Moustache hopped into the Astra and followed her back to the Falls Road.

***

Fergal McConville had served six-years in the H-blocks of the Maze Prison; or Long Kesh, as it is known by the nationalist community of the North; as the Maze Prison was built on the old Long Kesh air field, what with it's nissen huts, was used as a makeshift prison to hold the 'Internees' in 1971; his crime was possession of firearms and membership of the IRA.

"We missed him by two-minutes Fergal." Spike Currie spoke with frustration as Fergal McConville shook his head.

"Are you sure it was Loughlin," said McConville who pushed his silver-rimmed glasses up his nose with the middle finger of his left hand, then ran the palm of his right hand up his forehead and over his jet-black hair. His hair had been styled and cut in a top city centre salon, not the corner barbershop used my most volunteers of the IRA. Since his release from the 'Kesh' (Maze Prison), McConville had kept a lower profile in the IRA. He looked after the finances of the Belfast Brigade and looked every bit the man about town. He wore designer clothes and shoes; had an apartment away from the Falls Road and he drove a BMW.

The IRA financed his lifestyle, he fronted their pubs and clubs and wasn't shy when it came to enforcing at the 'deniable' racketeering that goes on at the numerous building sites around Belfast. He ran the gaming machines in the licensed premises and arcades around the city. So much IRA money passed through his hands that they turned a blind-eye to the entrepreneurial empire he had with Mary McAuley. McConville was tall, well built, and handsome, like Conor; but unlike Conor he was a cold-blooded killer.

"Oh aye it was him alright," said Currie, "Patrick Nugent's young brother, Fra, seen him going into Mary McAuley's flat."
"Jesus Christ!" said McConville, as he stroked his chin.

"Most of the boys were at a staff meeting and by the time they were told he was in the area and got a gun organised, Mary had taken him out of the district again."
"Why didn't they lift him when he came out of the flat? If I got him away I'd fix his wagon for him big-time."

"There were six of the younger ones waiting to grab him but he had something in his jacket. They're sure he was carrying, so they couldn't make a move because the weapon hadn't arrived yet."
"Where the fuck is Mary now?"
"She's back in her flat by herself." Currie carried on.

"Fergal, you were in charge of that purge against the IPLO in 94, you even put yourself on the line and done O'Neill yourself. Loughlin's one of the instigators of all

that, it doesn't look good on you that he's in the flat with *your girl*."
"Listen, I'll explain the facts of life to Mary. If he's still in Belfast, she'll get him back to the Falls and I'll give him his fuckin' medicine."

"Fergal, it'd be better if we could lift him and take him away. Don't forget, all you prisoners are out of jail now with the peace process, I'm sure Patrick Nugent would want to talk to the bastard that took his ma's leg off."

"I'll see ya the marra. I'm away to let Mary know that my two friends Mr Smith and Mr Wesson aren't too happy about her behaviour. I've a funny feeling she'll see things our way."
"Slán leát." (goodbye in Irish).
"Slán." McConville left for Mary's flat.

***

Victoria Dixon had left university and taken her first job with the government, she felt a job with the Civil Service was beneath her, having left college with an honours degree in Politics, Economics and Social Sciences. Quite by chance she met the late Mr. Simpson her tutor and mentor who immediately recognised her cunning ability to read situations and the sly underhanded way she was able to deal with people and manipulate them to her own advantage. He soon introduced her to the murky world of military intelligence and the SIS.

The phone-call was patched through to her home number.

"You may speak freely," said Dixon, "this is a secure line."

"Well," said Crew Cut, "Loughlin has just been dropped off at the hotel by a woman."
"Yes?"
"My man has a trigger on her now, to make sure the car goes to where it's registered."
"Have you done a 'P check' on the vehicle?"
"Just this minute, it's registered to a Mary McAuley at an address on the Falls Road."
"Who is she then?" asked Dixon.
"She's originally from Newry, so she must know him well, and she had connections with the IPLO back in the early 90's."
"I think we are getting warm." Although Crew Cut couldn't see it, Dixon was smiling as she lifted her glasses and used them to hold back her hair.

"If Loughlin was on the Falls Road tonight, he's either completely stupid, has balls to burn, or was there for the coke."
"I think the latter, don't you." said Dixon.
"If my man tells me that that car parks up on the Falls Road, I'd say you could take that to the bank."
"Excellent!" Dixon carried on. "If that cocaine is there I want it destroyed, and anyone else, like Loughlin, who is in the house also."
"It's a maisonette."
"OK, wait until Loughlin comes to collect it and make it look like an IRA bomb factory. We'll discredit Murphy

afterwards. She'll be back in prison, but on the other side of the bars."

"My man's back now, he's got his thumb up."

"Excellent! Everything you need will be delivered to you ASAP; keep me posted."

"Oh yeah!" said Crew Cut, "We lost Gorman in Dublin."

"Yes, I've just heard. But I wouldn't call it 'lost' he was always going anyway. That was well done; there will be a bonus in it for you two, as I said, keep me posted."

"What?" said Crew Cut, but she had already hung-up.

***

During the 'troubles', as the conflict in the North of Ireland is called by the people of Northern Ireland; the Europa Hotel was the most bombed building in the world; but it was never structurally damaged and survived the whole campaign. It now carries an air of 'elite,' as a place to say you stayed in Belfast. It is a splendid five-star with a bistro bar, restaurant, public bar and nightclub. The front of the building is like a wall of dark glass. A concierge stands suited and booted at the revolving door. Conor slipped him a five-pound-note as he passed.

"Good evening sir, how's your beautiful wife tonight?"

Conor smiled and nodded as he walked towards the elevator, his left hand in his pocket keeping a tight grip on the coke.

The foyer is large with high ceilings with the entrance to the bar at the window to the left; the restaurant is to the right. A young couple sat timidly on one of the plush settees, which gave impressive views of the marble staircase and balconies, awaiting their room as a bellboy loaded their bags onto a trolley. The young man took a handful of the complimentary mints as if he was getting something for nothing.

Conor could hear a fat, drunk American being obnoxious to the receptionist who answered with, "I'm sorry I couldn't be of more help Sir," and gave him an 'I-don't-give-a-fuck' smile as the concierge made his approach.

The elevator bell gave a 'ding' and the brass/gold coloured doors opened and the reflection of the fat American was gone. Conor pressed the button for the top floor and was now in a room of mirrors. A computer-generated, female, American voice announced, "Top floor, executive suite." Conor turned right and passed a sign above a double oak door that read 'Clinton Suite'. 'That must be where the president stayed in 1995', he thought, 'I'm going to get that room for Julie, when we get this few quid.'

A swipe of a plastic card and a green light told that the door was open. The room was big and decorated in oak furniture. Soft cushions were scattered on a king-size bed. Heavy velvet curtains hung around the window that gave a view of Belfast, across the city to the docks, where the Harland and Wolfe Cranes and the new Waterfront Hall set magnificent views across the sea.

Conor stumbled back and fell onto bed, as he could only take half a step because his trousers were around his ankles when Julie pushed him. She grabbed his jacket and climbed on top of him, her hair washed over him and he was in her mouth. And the heat. Her tongue, and her lips, and her teeth; and she was away again.

"You'll not be needing that," she said as she threw the cocaine on the bed-side table. Then she was back again. She slapped Conor's hands away, as he tried to grab her, then slapped him harder when he slapped her back.

"I'm still your officer, Conor Loughlin."
"OK Miss Murphy."

She pulled his head back and bit his hair as she kissed the top of his head. He felt warm skin on his face as she pressed her breast against him and her nipple closed his eye. Her hand tickled the inside of his thigh and her weight was off him. He wanted to scream, shout, explode; he felt so furious, so exposed. Then he was in her and she was on him again and she let him touch and find her.

"Keep your legs down Conor." She tickled him again and he rose to the ceiling, "Do as you're told." She slapped him harder. The TV flickered in the corner. She moved with a rhythm that was cruel and wonderful. She surprised him, she taunted him, and he surrendered. Then she would stop as she held him down, to let him know that she was in control the torturer, the mistress – if she wanted – and then she whispered in his ear. "Did you lock the door Conor? What would you do if they walked in and caught us?"

"Who, the hotel staff?"

She moaned.

"The police?"

She screamed.

"MI5?"

She threw her head back.

"The IRA?"

"Yes!"

"The IPLO?"

"YESSSSS!"

"THE WHOLE FUCKIN' LOT OF THEM?"

They came together and her nails scratched his chest.

The news came on the TV.

"A body has been found in Ballymun Flats in Dublin. Initial reports suggest it is a man who has suffered gunshot wounds to the head."

"PAT!"
Conor screamed and Julie lay back and cried.

15

Divis Flats is situated at the bottom of the Falls Road, Belfast. When the complex was originally built it was the answer to the growing housing shortage in West Belfast. It is a vast area on the outskirts of the City Centre, bordered by Divis Street, which runs a short distance to become the Falls Road, the Grosvenor Road, Albert Street and the West Link Motorway. The latter joins the M1 and M2 motorways and runs through Belfast separating Divis Flats from the City Centre.

Like most flat complexes in Britain, it suffered great depravation, and with the violence and unemployment in war-torn Belfast, it soon joined Ballymun as one of the 'upmarket' ghettos. It would be fair to say that a considerably large portion of the population turned to crime to escape poverty and in-turn, the IPLO, who they used to 'cover their backs' from the IRA, who frowned on anti-social behaviour. It was a strong hold for the IPLO until the IRA 'Night of the Long Knives' purge against them, in which Conor's friends were given their 'medicine'.

The flats are now knocked down and replaced by modern housing, which seems to be occupied by a 'better class of hooligan'. The IRA still have their tight grip, it is after all the Falls Road, and Mary's empire was flourishing.

She ran it in the shadow of St. Paul's Cathedral that towered over the block of maisonettes that stood in Albert Street. If the maisonettes had stood on the other side of the cathedral they would have been demolished along with the other flats, but stand they did, while St Paul's towered majestically above them.

Fergal McConville parked his BMW in the cathedral car park that gave a clear view of the maisonettes. Old habits die-hard and he checked the area for possible attack, up the stairway and along the dimly lit balcony.

A dog barked as McConville crossed the street and he put a hand into his coat as a car screeched at the corner then indicated left and spun up the Falls Road. He stepped over and around a dustbin and made sure not to tread on the shit-stained nappy that had spilt its contents, along with the rubbish, onto the stairway where the dog had been eating.

The stairway smelt of ammonia, where some drunk must have relieved the pressure on his bladder, and a 'pavement pizza' with the obligatory carrots, graced the top of the stairs. The drunk obviously thought the balcony needed a makeover. The balcony light flickered as McConville knocked Mary's door.

"Bout ye Mary!"

"Well," said Mary, her Newry accent gave a quiver. "It's not like you to call at this time of the night, big lad." She turned and walked to the living room; McConville followed her.

"Where is he?"

"Who?" Mary sat down.

"Listen you!" McConville now had her by the throat. "Conor Loughlin."

"What are ya talking about Fergal?" Mary had her two hands around his wrist pushing his arm back a bit, so she could breathe.

"I'll blow the fuck out of ye if ya keep tellin' me lies." said McConville as he rammed a gun between her legs.

"Nigh me and Mr Nine Millimetre here, we don't like you tellin' us these fuckin' lies." He pushed the gun firmer between her thighs.

"So let me explain the facts of life to ya. First I'll tell ya the good news, and then the bad news. The good news is; if you don't tell me what I want to know, I'm gonna fuckin' kill ya. The bad news is; I'm gonna torture you first. Ya see those baby blue eyes of yours? Well first I'm gonna put some battery acid in the left one, and leave it to melt on ya. Then I'm gonna let ya walk about town with it and you're gonna have to look at it in the mirror every day for a year, crying over your milky white eye.

Then after a year, I'm gonna melt the other one. Then after another year of trying to walk about blind, you'll be begging for the good news."

"Oh that Conor Loughlin! He's in the Europa."

***

"We've got to make our move fast," said Crew Cut. "Some of 'The Regiment' (SAS) boys can drop off what we need, where we need it, but first let's get into that maisonette and find the charlie, there's only one place it can be. If it's there, up she goes."

"What will we need to get in then?"
"Fuck all; we'll just knock the door. What did Dixon say? 'Anybody that is in the place is going anyway'."
"Let's do it!" said Moustache. They got into the Astra.

***

"What was he doing here Mary?" McConville put the gun into his waistband and ruffled Mary's hair with his other hand as though nothing had happened.

"You were going to shoot me. You pig!"
"Ah Mary! You know the craic yourself. Let's just call Mr Nine Millimetre a bit of an attitude adjuster."
"You pig!"
"What was he doing here?" Although McConville was smiling, Mary knew the threat was deadly serious.
"He said he just called to say hello. Nothing happened!"
"I don't give a fuck about that. What did he want?"

"Nothing. He was just talkin' about old times."
"I'm fuckin' tellin' ya nigh Mary! McConville was still on his feet and had his finger pointed right in Mary's face. She had seen that gesture all too often and knew what would be coming next.

'Buy myself a little bit of time,' Mary thought, 'they wouldn't go into the City Centre to try and get him.' "Ok," she said, "he wants me to meet him in the Europa tomorrow night."

"Good girl." McConville took off his glasses, sat down, and wiped them with a green satin cloth that he took from the lapel pocket of his cashmere overcoat. "You do that, and then get him back here till I find out what he wanted."

"He might want me to stay there, Fergal."
"If you have to stay, you have to stay. But you make sure that he calls to see ya before he leaves town. I don't care how you do it, but you *will* do it, if you know what's good for ya. OK love? McConville rubbed his eye with a menacing smile before putting his glasses back on, and Mary swallowed hard.
"OK."

"Nigh listen." McConville was back on his feet. "You dress yourself up real sexy."
"Like I would go out like a tramp!"
"Shut your mouth ya cheeky fuck. You better not fuck this up."
"Sorry Fergal." Mary put her hands up to protect herself.

"Mary I'm fuckin' tellin' ya nigh, people know he's here. So you wear one of those wigs you've got, I don't want anybody recognising ya with him."

"OK," said Mary as she went to get her stuff.

"Leave your car here you can stay with me tonight and think of Conor." He slapped her on the arse as she passed him.

'Cheeky fucker! I'll deal with Conor tomorrow,' she thought as she climbed the stairs. 'Just keep this maniac calm tonight.'

"And Mary, we'll get a taxi down tomorrow, he doesn't know me so I can stand at the bar and watch. I don't want anybody seeing my car outside the Europa."

"For fuck's sake!" Mary said under her breath, as she lifted her black wig.

***

The dog was still barking when the Village People climbed the stairway and manoeuvred around the pavement pizza.

"Dirty bastards!" said Crew Cut as he stepped around the vomit.

"Did you see that BMW?" asked Moustache as they came to Mary's door.

"Yeah, nice wasn't it? No wonder he drove off fast. He must be lost."

Two more steps and Crew Cut knocked the door, then knocked it again. Moustache looked over the balcony.

"Give it another go mate, her car's still here." Crew Cut looked through the letterbox and told Moustache that there must be no one home, as there were no coats on the hangers and the lights were out.
"Right," said Moustache, "we'll just have to go in."

The lock was a basic pin tumbler, a Yale lock, not the sort of security you would expect in Divis, but who was going to break into Mary McAuley's place, knowing the kind of company she kept.

"I know where the key is," said Crew Cut as he went to the turned-over bin and lifted a broken broom-handle.
"So much for technology." said Moustache.

Crew Cut opened the letterbox and put his hand through. He then put the broom-handle through, which was about two-and-a-half feet long, and held it by the end. The other end he held vertically up and manoeuvred it around until it touched the bottom of the lock, an inch up and there was the handle. A slight push and it was as if his fingers extended and turned the handle. "Open sesame," he said as the door opened.

The smell of coffee still hung in the air and a slice of half-eaten toast lay on the draining board by the sink.

"We must have just missed her." Moustache finished off the toast.

The cocaine wasn't hard to find, as the corner of the carpet lay over the green drapes, and Crew Cut was quick to order his gear from HQ.

"OK mate, I've spoken to Dixon and this is how she wants it done. The bomb is to be made here so it will take us a few hours."
"What if she comes back?"
"Well her fate is sealed now, anyone who comes in that door now is getting tied-up, they will just be written-off as a part of the IRA bomb team."
"No problem."
"The Regiment boys will leave a Transit-van outside within the hour. Everything that we need will be inside."
"Yes it's the dead of night; no-one will see fuck all."
"Even if they do, they'll think we are the IRA anyway. No problem." Crew Cut put the kettle on.
"There's some amount of coke here."
"There will be fuck-all left of anything when this lot goes up." They sat in the dark and awaited the Transit.

The shit-stained nappy and the pavement pizza had long since disappeared, along with the barking dog, when the Transit parked beside Mary's car. The Village People gave the SAS ten minutes, although they only needed seconds to slip back into the night, and then unloaded the Transit-van.

"Where the fuck did they get an industrial coffee grinder at this time of night." asked Moustache as they unloaded the ingredients onto Mary's kitchen floor.

"Look down the inside of it; it's been used for this before."
"Mad innit?"

Moustache opened the bags and Crew Cut did the mixing. Two fifty-kilo bags of commercial fertiliser, the one the farmers use, that come in little pellets.

First Crew Cut got the fertiliser pellets and ran them through the coffee-grinder to make a fine powder. Then, in a large plastic container, the powder was mixed with nitrobenzene, diesel oil and a little bit of this and some of that, all stuff that can be bought in your local supermarket. He now mixed it all together to make a nice concoction, like a smelly cake mixture and put it into black bin-liners. There was now over two hundred pounds of home made explosives, the same mix as was used to blow-up Canary Warf. It was not volatile enough to go off by its self, it needed some high explosive to create the shock wave, and just like the IRA would do, the Village People used Semtex. They used a kilo of the stuff, which was a bit of an over kill, but so was a two-hundred-pound fertiliser bomb. The Semtex was put in the mix with a commercial detonator. Crew Cut used a digital transmitter, so only he, and not some lunatic with a mobile phone or CB radio, could set of the charge. After checking for comms (communications between the remote control in his hand and the other bits that would be attached to the detonator), he fitted it to the bomb.

"We'll wait on her coming back," said Crew Cut, "deal with her, and then wait on Loughlin."
"We'll have to get a trigger back on Loughlin."

"Yeah, we may have to split-up for a bit, but this will come together quickly."

Waiting all day in the comfort of Mary's flat was no problem for the Village People. These were men who had been on opps all over the world, sometimes lying out in the rain for days keeping a trigger on a target. So watching MTV on mute was a walk-in-the-park and if Mary and Conor came in at the same time, their job was over.

Crew Cut checked his watch. It said 1900 hours, and no sign of Mary.

"Listen mate." He woke Moustache from his sleep. "I don't know what smells worse, that bomb or your farts."
"Fuck-off!" Moustache rubbed his eyes. "What is it?"
"I'm going back to watch the Europa."
"OK."
"If anyone comes, deal with them." He handed Moustache a nine-millimetre Browning High Power.
"If push comes to shove, we'll lift Loughlin and bring him here ourselves. Keep your phone on." Crew Cut went to the car; Moustache went and put the kettle on.

***

It was 19:55 when Mary pulled on her black wig. She had spent over an hour brushing it and giving it a good going over with a set of crimpers. She did her make-up a bit on the pale side, her eyes dark with red lipstick. She wore a black dress that clung to every curve of her body, a red button at the neck and an oval-shaped hole at the front that revealed her cleavage. Her tiny waist carried a red belt and tanned legs with red Bally-Marilyn shoes. The look was altogether quite gothic.

"You look… different," said McConville, "strange, but you're a cracker."
'Is that supposed to be a complement you prick.' Mary thought. "Thanks." she said as she lifted her long black coat.

"Nigh listen Mary, he won't be able to resist you girl. So you get him back to the flats tonight."
"What if he wants me to stay, Fergal?"
"You say you have to go home. Make him want ya. If he doesn't come back tonight, he'll be thinkin' of ye all night. He'll be up for some of ya the marra. I know I would." He slapped her ass and she screwed up her face. "You go into the hotel from the side entrance; I'll go in from the front." A car sounded its horn three times and they left to get into the taxi.

McConville left his overcoat in the cloakroom and stood at the bar beside Conor. They didn't make eye contact, McConville knew, the eyes give everything away, if he looked Conor in the eye, Conor would know something was wrong.

The bar had a few people in it and Crew Cut was under pressure to keep track of who was who. Mary stopped when she saw McConville and Conor standing beside each other, then gave herself a mental slap and walked over and kissed Conor on the cheek.

"Jul… fuck Mary! I thought you were someone else, you look different… you look great!"

"Some things never change." She said as she lifted Conor's chin to remove his eyes from her cleavage.

"Talk to ma face boy."

"I've made my choice," he giggled," Only windin' ya up babe." Conor led her to a table by the window.

'Excellent,' thought McConville.

'Excellent, he's with Murphy,' thought Crew Cut.

The conversation was back to Newry and old times, then the IPLO and work, Mary's work got a mention; then Conor told her about the cocaine.

"What! You fuckin' bastard!"

"Mary, for fuck sake! We were all young and foolish back then."

"You must have thought I was a real stupid dickhead."

"Mary, hold on. Calm down." Mary *was* in control, she didn't raise her voice but her mannerisms had changed.

"Mary you worked for the boys too, they told *us* what to do."

"And what would happen to me if that had a been caught?"

"How would it have got caught?"

"Sure the whole organisation was littered with touts."

"Only four of us knew where it was, and the rest are all dead."

"Conor, you fuckin' bastard! That's why you're here; to use me again; to get your stuff out."

"Mary, you're not getting used. My mate was supposed to come from Dublin today to help me. But there's a bit of trouble there, so you're going to have to help me. You and Julie."
"Nigh who the fuck is Julie?"
"She's my girl, she's here with me."
"Ah for fuck sake Conor."

Conor then went on to tell briefly about Julie.
"You listen to me Loughlin. You've caused me a world-load of trouble since you came back."
"What do you mean?"
"Conor, the Ra know you're here, you better get me out of this." Mary was angry, but was on the verge of crying.
"Mary you'll be well looked after out of this, and you won't have to do that job any more."
"Conor, I'm trying to keep composed, there's one of them watching us."
"You're a dirty bastard Mary!"
"Don't look round ya prick! I'm going to have to take him back to mine tonight; he'll want to know all that we talked about."
"What are ya goin'a say?"
"I don't fuckin' know? You give me your room number and I'll phone ya in the morning. You better get me out of this!" She stood up and gave him a kiss. "Tell Julie I said hello." She said sarcastically as she put on her coat.

Conor and Mary walked to the foyer where they mingled with the revellers, pretending all was fine, then kissed again and Conor walked to the elevator, past the cloakroom where McConville was collecting his coat.

***

The phone vibrated three times before Moustache answered. The back-light on the screen was set on low. "Yes mate." MTV still flickered in the corner.
"Any sign of McAuley?"
"No, there's been a few knocks at the door but no sign of her all day, how's things with you?"
"Loughlin's just got his coat and Murphy and him are leaving the hotel, he's just called a taxi so I'll put a tail on him. You sit tight."
"No problem."

***

McConville pulled up the collar of his cashmere coat and Mary pushed the button to open the telescopic umbrella. True to form, it was raining in Belfast. Mary stared out into the night; two drunks fought outside the pub, as the crowd jeered them on, laughing at their antics. An equally drunken woman in her mid-twenty's exposed her left breast as the boob tube she wore to complement her red mini-skirt got pulled down as she tried to separate them. The crowd roared again. Mary didn't notice them as the taxi turned into Divis Street.

"Fergal."
"Shush!" He put his finger to his lips and nodded towards the taxi driver. "You can tell me all back at the flat."
'Oh fuck!' Thought Mary.

***

The phone vibrated again.

"Yes mate?"

"Listen mate!" There was a sign of urgency in Crew-Cut's voice. "Get ready. Looks like they're heading your way, I'm right behind them."

Moustache put the hands-free unit into the phone, the speaker firmly into his ear; he clipped the phone to his belt.

"We're on The Falls now," said Crew-Cut, "and turning onto Albert Street. They must have a key, get out of the flat and we'll detonate as soon as they're in the place. I'll be in the church car park.

Moustache took a quick look around the room to make sure that nothing was left behind. He put on his jacket, lifted the Browning pistol and checked the chamber to make sure there was a round in the breach and ready to fire, if needed. He knew that it was, but it always made him feel better to check. He placed the gun in the waistband of his jeans, but didn't zip-up his coat; he used the Velcro strips he had attached that were easy to pull open in case he needed a quick-draw. He then lifted the remote control for the bomb, checked comms once more, and put it into his jacket pocket.

The smell of the bomb was now giving him the mother of all headaches, so he swallowed the last two of Mary's Ibuprofen that he'd found in the kitchen beside the toast. He opened the front door. A red baseball cap with the symbol of the San Francisco 49ers made him snigger, as he thought of how much it looked like the Sinn Fein emblem. 'Kind of ironic.' he thought. As he was about to walk out of the door, he noticed a plaque on the wall declaring the proclamation of Ireland by the Provisional Government of Ireland in 1916 and read:

> *We declare the right of the people of Ireland to the ownership of Ireland and to the unfettered control of Irish destinies, to be sovereign and indefeasible...*

"Hurry up mate!" The hands-free crackled in his ear, "they're in the car park."

He put on the cap and pulled it down so the peak covered most of his face when he looked down. He could hear the taxi door close as he shut the door. He moved quickly and Crew-Cut gave a running commentary of their targets movements.
"They're at the foot of the stairs mate." And Moustache could hear the wind catch the umbrella.

Two tanned female legs in high-heels and a pair of men's Italian loafers was all Moustache saw of them as he dropped his head and squeezed past them on the stairs.
"Sorry mate," he said in his bad Belfast accent.
McConville stopped and watched him from the top of the stairs. 'Who the fuck was that?' he thought and carried on up the balcony after Mary.

Mary opened the door, stopped and hung her coat on the hangers in the hall.

"What's that smell?" She said as she took off her black wig and hung it on the banister. "Smells like marzipan, you would think someone was baking a cake in here."

MTV flickered away in the corner as McConville turned on the lights and the all-too-familiar smell of nitro-glycerine, that marzipan-smell given off by the reaction between the nitrobenzene and fertiliser; hit him right in the face. He didn't even try to run, as his life flashed briefly before his eyes and the souls that he had sent before him, stood in the corner and waited for him.

"OUT MARY! BOMB! BOMB! BOMB!"

He shouted as the red light flashed on the detonator.

***

"Jesus Christ!" said Crew-Cut. "Where did she come from?"
"Who?" asked Moustache as he made his way across the church car-park.
"McAuley, she's running on the balcony."
"What shall I do?"
"Detonate for fucks sake!

***

For the briefest of moments there was silence. A beautiful, terrible silence. Not even Mary's footsteps could be heard as she ran barefoot along the balcony. A silence spawned by the devil.

It was broken by a crack as the shock wave came first, breaking windows and buckling the metal railings of the balcony. Mary was thrown down the stairwell and landed on the overturned bin. The shock wave lifted Moustache and launched him over the bonnet of the Astra, ripping his buttocks and puncturing his eardrums. And then the bang. A sonic boom that broke windows for a square mile, and the intense, white flash of light that created a vacuum as the explosion sucked all the oxygen away. Then a second crack as the aftershock ignited the ruptured underground gas main. The orange and blue flames mingled and intertwined like fingers. The fire lit up the sky. The flames were rising licking the clouds. McConville and the family in the maisonette below, with the Kerry-Blue Terrier and the pair of budgies, were atomised.

***

Rapping noises and then a thud as debris rained down on the Astra in a rhythmical cluster tapped out by a dead man.

Moustache dragged himself to his feet and then to the Astra where Crew-Cut was already on the phone to Dixon.

"Jesus Christ! It went up like a tinder-box." He selected first gear and squeezed the car through the gates of the Chapel car park, trying to manoeuvre around the rubble. Lights were coming on in homes and people were beginning to filter onto the streets as Crew-Cut mounted the kerb to avoid the roaring gas-main.

"Are the principles eliminated?" asked Dixon.
"Oh yes, Loughlin and Murphy were in the place, they're gone. There's a good chance that McAuley got it too. She was running on the balcony when it went off."
"I'm not worried about her" Dixon carried on. "She's only a victim of circumstance. That's a good job, well done!"
"Fuck me, my ears!" Moustache was bending over with both hands, cupping his ears as Crew-Cut selected third gear and pulled onto the Falls Road.

A black taxi that was taking the remnants of the crowd that had jeered on the fight; took out the back end of the Astra as it pulled across the junction of Albert Street and the Falls Road. It sent it spinning into the wall of the old Conway Street Mill. The windscreen went out and Moustache was once again across the bonnet. Crew-Cut slumped across the steering wheel. Dixon was cut of as the battery came out of the phone.

***

People ran in all directions screaming about the poor family. Then someone found Mary, unconscious but alive, at the bottom of the stairs. The people in the Taxi went to help the people in the Astra. Spike Currie was already there with his boys.

Someone tried to administer CPR to Moustache and as he tried to turn him onto his back the Browning pistol fell from the waistband of his jeans. The man stopped and shouted for Currie. The crowd gathered and became angrier as Currie searched him and found the remote-control in his pocket.

Crew-Cut started to come round and switched on immediately when he saw a high- profile Republican figure screaming orders at the crowd. Crew-Cut drew his pistol and took off the safety catch as the crowd started to attack the car. Broken house bricks and pieces of railings were used to smash the windows and a man with a railing was on top of the Astra flailing away at the windows when Crew-Cut discharged a round. For a moment the crowd ran away and Crew-Cut tried to climb out of the window to make his escape. The man on the roof hit him on the head with the bar.

Crew-Cut and Moustache were bundled into the taxi and taken to the Falls Park, where they were stripped and searched. Spike Currie personally put two bullets in the back of their heads.

16

The rain rattled off the window and the wind whipped the walls. Conor and Julie lay watching the storm in the dark.

"Conor!" Julie snuggled closer. "That thunder is very loud."
"Aye. You're right. It's a bit loud for thunder." Conor sat up on the bed.
"What Conor?" Julie sat up and looked worried; the covers slid off her. Conor just looked.
"What?" She asked.
"Nah nothin', the war's well over." He covered her ample breasts with his chest as they lay back.
"It nearly put the windys in big lad." She took off his accent.
"Did you think the IRA were going to blow us up?"
"Ahh… Conor."
"Or maybe the IPLO?"
"Ohh… Conor."
"Is it doing it for you again Miss Murphy?"
"It always will Conor."
"The British fuckin' army?"
"Conorrrrrrr!"
They kissed deeply and the blankets were off them.

***

"Conor! Conor wake up, there's someone at the door."

"It's probably the maid."

"No Conor, they have the key."

"The rooms OK, call back later!"

"Loughlin, you open this fuckin door!"

"Jesus Christ Julie, it's Mary." Conor ran naked to open the door.

"Put some clothes on for fuck sake." Mary walked into the room and on into the bathroom where she found the bathrobe and threw it out to Conor. Conor shrugged his shoulders and smiled at Julie as he put it on.

"What's wrong?" He said. "What time is it anyway?" Mary stared at herself in the bathroom mirror as Conor watched from the open door. Her black dress looked a mess and the rain had soaked and clapped her short, bleach-blonde hair against her head. Her dark eye-makeup was smudged and looked like the tears on a painted clown as it ran down her cheek. She had no shoes on.

"What the fuck happened to you? And what are you doing with one shoe in your hand?"

"I don't know." She dropped a red, high-heel on the floor. "I kicked the other one off in the hall but I had to pull that one off with my hand because I couldn't run."

"What the fuck are you on about?" He walked and sat on the bed beside Julie.

"The bomb Conor."

Julie looked at Conor and made a puzzled face as they heard the shower go on.

"Bomb! What fuckin' bomb? Are you taking drugs?"

"My flat Conor, it blew up."

"What!" Conor ran into the bathroom followed by Julie, who by now had rapped the blanket around herself. Conor caught Mary just before she fainted in the shower, fully clothed, and carried her soaking wet to the bed.

"Poor girl." Julie turned on the bedside-lamps and put the kettle on. Mary's dress was soaked though and she was going into shock. Julie went into the bathroom and put on the other dressing gown and came back with the blanket.

"Conor, finish making that hot drink, and I'll get that dress off her." Julie stripped Mary and started to dry Mary with a large, soft, white bath-towel. There were only slight grazes on her head but Mary gave a moan as Julie opened a cut on her forehead. The towel was now a mixture of red, dirt and make-up; like a watercolour any five-year-old would be proud of.

"You're OK sweetheart," said Julie, as she pulled one of her night-dresses over her head.

"You must be Julie; bet you didn't think you would be needing this," said Mary as she helped pull down her night-dress. Julie just smiled and wrapped her in the blanket.

"Got to keep you warm babe." said Conor as he handed her a cup-of-tea.

"Conor, I don't know what happened. He just told me to run and I couldn't go fast cos my dress was too tight. And I was really scared Conor. And then there was this big bang and I fell down the stairs and the bin was all smelly and everything. And there was all this heat and dust, and everybody was shouting, and I was scared Conor. And I just ran away Conor, and I was scared. And, and, and…" Mary was hyperventilating.

"Shhh it's alright nigh."

"But Conor, my head's sore and everything, so it is."

"I know love, I'll have to keep you awake for a couple of hours in case you've got concussion, but you'll be alright. We'll sort this out in the morning." Mary put her head on Julie's shoulder and started crying. Julie held her.

***

"Jesus Christ Julie! What are we goin'a do nigh?" They talked in the bathroom after letting Mary sleep. "We've about five-hundred quid left and a kilo of coke."

"What's that worth?"

"About thirty grand, but we can't take that back to England; it would last no time."

"Wait until we see what Pat has to say; he may be able to work something out."

"Pat! You don't seem to have grabbed the concept Julie, Pat's dead."

"We don't know that for sure Conor, the body hasn't been named yet."

"That's cos they don't know who the fuck it is yet Julie. Them Dublin bastards have fixed his wagon."

"Fixed his wagon?" said Julie. The last time she heard that Pat had said it. "Conor, Pat didn't kill Dominic did he?"

"What do you think Julie? Do you think this is a fuckin' game?"

"You're swearing a lot Conor."

"Julie; that fat faggot let out 'the secret'. He caused all this. For every action there is an equal and opposite reaction. Didn't *you* tell me that? Well Pat knew it. Pat knew how bad this was going to get, but we had no other option. We spun our money and took our chance. And we lost."

"Don't say that Conor. The glass is not half-empty it's half-full. Give Pat one more day. If he doesn't show, we'll think of something. We have to."

Julie took Conor's face in her hands and kissed him deeply.

"I love you Conor."

"Oh Julie, I love you too."

"Do you think the Police will be looking for us?"

"Julie we can't, Mary's just gone to sleep."

"*She* won't be looking for us, will she?" She bit his ear lobe and pressed him hard against the sink.

***

"Conor sat on the chair with his back to the window, holding his head in his hands, as Mary recalled the night's events.

'We were so close,' he thought, 'we had the ball at our feet and lost it.'

"Well girls." Conor got on his feet. "We've no other option but to go on with the plan."

"How can we do that?" asked Julie. "The coke was all destroyed."

"Aye, we know that but Taffy and his firm don't."

"Who's Taffy?" asked Mary.

"Gary, a Welsh lad I met in jail. He has a man who was going to buy the whole lot."

"We only have one kilo." said Julie.

"We'll do it like this." Conor ruffled Mary's hair as he walked past.

"I've already said that I won't show the coke until I see the million pounds, right?"

"Yeah."

"And they know that and have agreed to that. Right?"

"Carry on."

"Well, that kilo there, we show that as a sample and they'll be well-impressed."

"What about the rest?" Both girls asked at the same time.

"Well nigh," smiled Conor, "once we have the money in our car, we show them the stuff in the boot of another car."

"What stuff?" asked Julie.

"Glucose."

"What!" Both girls spoke again at the same time.

"We'll stick one-hundred kilos of glucose in the boot of a car."

"They wouldn't fall for that Conor." said Mary.

"They will. We'll have to pack it up the same way as the coke was packed, so when they open up the boot, all they'll see is one-hundred packages all taped-up. If they make a quick check with the knife they'll see white powder. After they get a couple of lines of the good stuff up their noses in our car, they won't know whether they've been blown-up or stuffed. The paranoia will be flying in and they'll just want that stuff out of there as quickly as possible."

"Conor, these are drug-dealers, these are dangerous people. Do you think it would work?" asked Mary as she played with the TV remote.
"It will have to. By the time they get a good look at it, we'll be well away with the few quid."
"You had better hope that stuff is as good as you think it is," said Julie as she pointed to the bedside cabinet. Conor went to the drawer and took out the coke.
"There's only one way to find out," he said as he pulled back the black insulation tape that Sean O'Rourke had placed there the day it all went pear-shaped. He took out a little piece about the size of a penny and crushed it with the plastic key-card. He chopped a line out, rolled up a twenty-pound note and sniffed it up his nose.

"Nigh that's what I'm talkin' about!" He turned and smiled at the girls as his body rushed with pleasure and oozed confidence. Nothing mattered anymore. He was 'the man.' How can anything go wrong? He was Conor Loughlin, he was with the two best-looking women this side of the Atlantic and he had fucked both of them. He was the best looking man in the world, owner of the body that brought tears to the fannies of every woman who ever as much as glanced at him, and he was about to become a millionaire.

"Give me a line of that." said Mary as she lifted the rolled-up note. Julie shook her head, but she wasn't angry, it had to be tested if they were going to get away with this.

"Want some?" Conor asked Julie.

"No babe... Yeah. Why not? In for a penny, in for a pound."

"I wish Pat was here," said Conor, as they competed to talk. "We'll put MTV on for a while, then turn back to catch the news later-on. We all deserve a little break."

"Yeah," said Julie, "I wish Pat was here." As they all took another line.

***

Time passed quickly. The hours flew as Conor and the girls planned their quest for world domination. Every problem in the world was sorted out and then some. And it was dark again. The 'do not disturb' sign had done its fair share of work today. As Mary surfed the channels, Sky News came on and they came back to Earth with a crash.

"Jeez Conor, look at my flat!" A news reporter stood in the middle of the street with what looked like a scene straight from Beirut, smouldering in the background. Rubble was everywhere. Mary's block of maisonettes was in ruins, in fact Mary's and the one below it were no longer there. Workers from the gas-company were working on the main and a spokesperson promised that power would be resumed as soon as possible. The reporter went on to interview the parish priest from St Paul's.

"Well it's been a terrible tragedy." The priest adjusted a strand of hair that had been flapping in the wind and wound it over his bald head like a walnut whip. He put a flat-cap on it to keep it in place. "I don't really know what happened myself. All I know is there was a huge explosion and I've been here all night and day looking for bodies; in-fact the whole district has been helping."
"What casualties do you know of father?"
"Well there was the poor Molloy family; they seem to have been sleeping when it happened."

"Oh God!" Mary put her hand to her mouth.

"And the wee McAuley girl who lived in the flat above."
"And no bodies have been recovered yet. Is that right father?" asked the reporter.
"I believe that to be correct. There are rumours that Mary McAuley was seen staggering about the street afterwards, but no one can, as of yet, confirm this. The police forensics, who you can see here," he pointed to a group of men in white overalls, "are saying they know for definite that there are at-least six casualties."
"Thank you father." The reporter switched back to the studio where a man and woman talked about the explosion.

"There is all sorts of speculation," said the woman, "what is your opinion Mr Boyd?"

John Boyd was the editor-in-chief of the Belfast Sunday Globe, the national Sunday newspaper. He had written countless articles on the Northern Ireland conflict, most of them biased towards the police, as a cousin of his was the Chief Constable. So he had a good insight into what was going on and he was a great outlet for police propaganda.

"Well as you say, there is a lot of speculation but the police are hinting towards an own-goal."
"Can you explain that please?"
"An IRA bomb factory. They may believe that this was a renewed assault to break the peace-process and that bomb went off in the manufacturing process. These kind of bombs are so volatile."
"I hear that the police have some definite suspects, can you confirm this?"
"No, I haven't heard, but I believe there will be a statement from police soon."
"Sinn Fein, the political wing of the IRA, will be holding a press conference at nine in the morning, to discuss the explosion; no doubt you will be there Mr Boyd?"
"I will."
The reporter turned to the camera.
"In a separate incident two bodies have been found with gunshot wounds to the head, three miles away in the Falls Park. Sky News will keep you posted as reports come in."

"Jesus girls it's bad," said Conor.
"I know; did you see my flat? What will I do?"
"You can't do anything; the Peelers will have you away quicker than a rabbit gets fucked."
"Conor!" said Julie.
"I'll tell ya what," said Conor. "You're lucky they didn't put your photo on the TV."
"I know," said Mary, but not really knowing why.

"Well, you know our plan, you know what we have to do; we'll just take another line of this to sort our heads out and then we'll try to get some sleep. We'll start work after the press conference in the morning."
"Do you think we should?" said Julie as she rolled up the note.

***

The ringing telephone woke Conor from his sleep. It only seemed like two minutes since he had ordered a wake-up call, but it was now 8.30am. He put the kettle on and walked out into the corridor, where the maid was cleaning the room opposite.

"Will you need your room serviced today, Sir?"
"Yeah, we're going out at about ten."
"I'll leave it until after that then."

Conor took some tea, coffee, milk and a handful of shortcake biscuits from her trolley. The maid gave him a weak smile as he closed the door. Conor made the tea, Julie had coffee and no one talked as they stared into their cups. They waited their turn for the shower.

'Is the high worth the payback,' thought Julie. They had another cup as they sat to watch the press conference.

The president of Sinn Fein sat at the microphone, to his right sat Spike Currie; to his left sat a pretty woman in her mid-thirties, who looked like a secretary but was in fact the president's assistant, Jaqui McGill. She took notes, deemed what members of the press should ask questions, whether or not it was an appropriate question to be asked; and whether or not it warranted an answer. The president spoke.

"I read this statement on behalf of the Irish Republican Army." The crowd jostled and jockied for position. "The IRA denies any part or involvement in the explosion at Albert Street." He went on to say how they categorically deny this and disenfranchise themselves from that; all political small talk. Then he produced photographs. "These are photographs of the weapons and remote-control the IRA recovered from the undercover army that the IRA arrested and executed at the scene of the explosion." The crowd went quiet. "A leading member of Sinn Fein and his girlfriend are believed to have lost their lives in the explosion. We believe that this is part of a British government, dirty-tricks department trying to discredit Sinn Fein and expel them from the new Northern Ireland Parliament."

"Jesus Christ!" said Conor as the news switched back to the studio. "This is getting really heavy."

And then another bomb dropped.

"A prisoner believed to be part of a renegade paramilitary, group escaped from HMP Longmoore, in England, with the help of a member of prison staff. These two are believed to be part of an organisation opposed to the peace-process and were planning a new campaign of terror on the British mainland." Julie dropped her cup. "Conor Loughlin, from Newry in Northern Ireland and Julie Murphy, who is of Irish decent are believed to have been in the apartment when it exploded." Their two photographs appeared on the screen.

***

"Oh my God, no...!" Cried Simone. "JULIE!"

***

"Excellent!" Smiled Dixon.

***

"For fuck sake!" Taffy shook his head.

***

Mrs Sharples cried.

***

"We've got to get the fuck out of here!" Said Conor.

***

After a quick gathering of thoughts Conor and the girls started to pack. They knew it would not be long before Conor and Julie were recognised by the hotel staff. They packed everything and gave the room a quick clean. Mary went to the corridor and spoke to the Maid.

"What are you doing Mary?" said Conor. "Nigh she's seen all of us!"

"You dick head! She works for me part-time. Do you think I came in the front door looking like I did last night. She'll get us out the service entrance and she won't say anything to anybody, ever. She's one of mine."

"Oh Mary, you're a diamond. Julie kissed her on the cheek and Conor slapped her ass. "Aheem, nice." Thought Mary as the colour flushed in her face. "Nah never."

As they moved towards the door, Conor stopped and walked back to the phone. He dialled nine for an outside line and then dialled a cell phone. The four rings seemed to take forever, then it answered.

"Gary it's Conor!"

"I thought..."

"Never mind what the news said, it was hairy as fuck, but I got away with the stuff."

"Good man boyo. What happened?"

"No time to talk nigh mate, I'll see you in three days at that pub car park we talked about. Alright?"

"Is Pat alright?"

"Nah, he's gone."

"I'm sorry Conor." Taffy lied.

"I know mate, that's the way it goes. Everything as I said it, no fuckin' about; you know how heavy our firm is, alright?"

"No problem Conor, for fuck sake, you don't even have to say that." Gary was smiling as he lied.

"Sorry mate, I'll phone ya in a couple of days."

"OK... Conor! How much stuff?"

"All of it."
"All of it?"
"Hundred big-ones.
"Brilliant."
They hung up.

Conor lifted his and Julie's bags Mary was dressed in a pair of Julie's jeans and a sweater. As Conor put his hands on the door-knob he stopped. A heavy bag with what sounded like it contained tools was being set down outside the door.
"What's that?" asked Mary.
"Shush!" Conor put his finger to his lips. "Maybe it's the Maid." He whispered as he took his Leatherman tool from his pocket and opened the knife-blade.
"Maybe it's the police."
"Ohh..." said Julie.
"No," whispered Conor, "they'd be straight in." He gestured for the girls to move back, took three deep breaths to oxygenate himself, turned the knob slowly then quickly opened the door and reached out into the hall.

17

Sav was a university graduate. He was tall, good-looking, with an athletic build. He had majored in English, Maths, etc. All the usual that is needed to become a teacher, his real passion was teaching sport, so he qualified with honours as a physical education teacher. On the field his large build could be intimidating; off the field his softly spoken middle-class voice could lull the foolhardy into a false sense of security, because Sav loved money. He soon realised that drugs were where the big money was to be made, and he was up to his neck in it. In the early 1990s Sav served a short prison sentence for possession of drugs; that's where he met his now partner-in-crime, Spooner; who was also in prison on a similar charge. The two emerged from prison eager to learn the drug trade properly, and even more determined not to get caught again. This is when Sav learned to kill. He did it, coldly, clinically and willingly. He was Savidge by name and savage by nature.

"So he's on his way with the gear then Taff? That's great news." Sav spoke as he casually flicked through the pages of Bodybuilding Monthly magazine. Spooner sat down with the Bud's.

"Yeah, that's right, and he says he's got a hundred kilos."

"Excellent," said Spooner, "and you know what? all that shit on the news about Ireland plays right into our hands. If they think they're already dead, then nobody will be looking for them. So let's not disappoint anyone. Right Taff?"

Gary nodded his head in approval.

"Now listen Gary," said Sav, "you've known us a long time and have earned good money with us, right."

"No problem Sav."

"Now this is different Gaz, there's a hundred kilos of coke here, after Spooner gets at it two-hundred keys at twenty five grand each. That's five million pounds. That's without even breaking it into ounces. Now remember this: you don't even know these people, you'll be able to retire after this."

"Yeah." said Taffy.

"Now this Conor, he doesn't know Spooner or me."

"Right."

"But he trusts you."

"Right."

"He knows Spooner owns the money so he'll expect him to have the briefcase full of cash."

"Right." Gary was taking all in.

"So Spooner won't be able to have a gun, but as I said, he trusts you, you'll have to have one to cover me.

"Why, where are you going to be?"

"I'll just be standing off-side. He'll want to look at the money in the car but we'll keep him outside. That's why I've chosen that car park; it's secluded."

"OK."

"Now, if he's happy he'll show the tester, and if we're happy he'll show the whole kit. When he does I'll come out and give them this." He produced a .357 Magnum revolver. "You make sure that Spooners behind you and give diagonal cross-fire if I don't drop them first time; which is unlikely."

"Thank God!"

"Are you alright with that mate?"

"Yeah, fuck 'em."

"Remember you'll be doing the talking, so don't give the game away."

"No problem I'm well up for it."

**

Conor and Julie didn't speak as they cruised along in the Ford Granada. They were too engrossed in thoughts of what was about to happen. They were flapping. The Granada was a hired job, hired in Liverpool using the hotel maid's credit card and driving license. After the overnight crossing on the Belfast to Liverpool ferry. Mary bluffed her way with the cards admirably. After all, a bit of fraud was nothing new to an ex-working girl. The odd chequebook and card were par-for-the-course when trade was a bit slow back in 1992.

It was 9.45 p.m. and the meeting was for 10.00 at a pub called the Hare and Hounds, near Tamworth in Staffordshire. The pub was a large country eating-house with and enclosed car park at the rear that could hold three hundred cars. People travelled from all over the Midlands to eat there, and although it was in the countryside, it was easy to find, as the country road that the pub was on was only ten minutes from the motorway.

Conor felt confident meeting there when Taffy suggested it. Taffy said it was a good halfway point. Conor's cousin Tom lives in Tamworth and it would be a quick run back to Tom's when they got the money. In reality it was Sav's idea to meet there, as he had a share in the pub, and after he'd 'whacked' Conor and Co. the bodies could be stored in the pub cellar while they waited for a safe time to move them to a friends pig-farm for disposal.

Pigs will eat anything. A couple very hungry pigs will eat a twelve-stone man in twenty minutes; bones and all. Of course, you have to cut the body into four, shave the hair and pull the teeth, as those are the only parts that will not digest. So for all intent and purposes, Spooner and the boys had a hot and heavy date planned for Conor and Co. with Pinky and Perky.

"Right Julie," Conor broke the silence. Mary should already be there in the other car, so we'll get them into our car and get them out of their heads, then, once we get the money we'll give the signal to Mary, who'll come walking from the other car."
"For God's sake Conor, how many times are we going to go over this?"
"Just making sure love."
"Conor, you know what to do, just do it."

It was 9.55 and Conor parked the Granada at the hedge at the back of the car park.

***

The weapon Sav chose was a Smith and Wesson .357 Magnum revolver. It looked similar to the .38 that Pat had used to kill Simpson, only it was a bit chunkier. It was a dark anthracite colour and had a rubber handle.

The ammunition was full metal jacket (lead covered in copper). Sav had scored a cross into the points of each of the six bullets that it held, to make them dumb-dumbs.

These bullets are lethal, as if a Magnum was not enough, dumb-dumbs break up upon entering the body, and spread in all directions. They 'do' every organ on impact. A .357 would take your arm off if it hit you on the shoulder, one hit from one of these dumb-dumbs and you were gone.

He gave Taffy a Walther PPK 9mm. This is a small semi-automatic that holds nine rounds. It's small and easy to conceal but packs a big punch. Although Taffy didn't know it, after Sav had dropped Conor and Co. Taffy and spooner were to put a bullet each, into the head of their bodies. This was Sav's insurance that nobody could talk about the killings; they'd all had a hand in it. Sav stood in the darkness watching from the shadow of the outbuilding that contained a children's play area, 'Thrills and Spills'. He had already checked his weapon, but did it again as he saw Taffy and

Spooner get out of the Merc with the case that contained £1,000,000 in cash.

***

"Well, here goes babe," said Conor as he got out of the Granada. The kilo of cocaine he kept tucked inside his jacket.
"I thought you were bringing them to the car?" said Julie.
"I am, I'll show them this first and then I'll come back with the money."
"Be careful Conor."
He nodded his head and closed the door.

Taffy and Spooner walked to the back of the Merc and waited by the boot. Spooner stood by the car as Taffy took a few steps towards Conor and shook his hand. He embraced him as old friends do, but really he was checking to see if Conor had a weapon. He didn't.

"Conor," said Gary, "this is my man, there's no need for introductions, let's get this done as quickly as possible. Where's the stuff?"
"Show me the money."
"My man's got it in the case, Conor. Where's the coke?"
Conor opened his jacket and produced the cocaine.
"I've a kilo here for you to look at, the rest is nearby; let me see the money."

Spooner sat the case on the boot-lid and opened the locks. The queen smiled up at Conor. The ambient orange glow of the car park lights seemed to catch the watermark on the notes and make them twinkle like embers on a log fire. Conor smiled back.

"Let's have a look at that," said Spooner.
"Come to the car and I'll cut a few lines out." Conor tried to walk away but Gary put his hand on him.
"No, stay in the open," said Spooner. "I want to see all around me."
'Oh fuck!' Thought Conor. He had no choice but to hand over the coke. "There you go."

Spooner closed the case and sat the kilo on top of it. He took out a piece about the size of your thumbnail and crumbled it on top of his thumbnail, which he held as if tossing a coin. He took a sniff.
"You too." said Conor to Gary, and he did, and Spooner smiled.

"FUCKING EXCELLENT! Where's the rest?"

Conor raised his hand and Mary got out of the blue Peugeot 505 Estate, with Irish number-plates.

"In the back of that." said Conor, as he put his hand on the case full of money.
"Wait until I have a look." Spooner ushered Mary to stand beside Conor and opened the tailgate of the Peugeot. Thirty seconds seemed like half-an-hour. Conor and Mary looked at each other then at the case, then at the Granada and Julie and then back at the money again. 'Could they make it? Would they make it? What the fuck, let's do it!'

Julie was already climbing into the driving seat as Conor grabbed the case.

"What the fuck!" Screamed Spooner. "You fucking bastards!" He ran from the back of the Peugeot with the bag of glucose. Conor had the case but Taffy had Mary. He had the pistol drawn and had Mary by the back of her hair. She tried to kick free, but Taffy slapped her across the back of the head with the Walther; she fell to her knees. Conor got to the passenger door just as Sav was pulling Julie screaming from behind the steering wheel. He too slapped her with his pistol and then pointed it at Conor.

"Get away from that fucking car; you cunt!"

Conor dropped the case, put his hands up and stepped back. There was a blue flash and his face was in a puddle beside the front wheel.

"Don't hurt him!" screamed Julie as Spooner stuck a size nine into his ribs just for good measure.
"Don't hurt him?" shouted Spooner, "I'll give you 'don't fucking hurt him!' "
"Calm down." Sav spoke softly, but his eyes were raging with fire. All three were dragged in front of the Granada, their kneeling shadows sprawled across the car park as the car headlights silhouetted them against the night-sky.
"Stand back," said Sav.

All Conor could hear was the Granada ticking over and Julie crying as she put her hands to her head. Conor tried to reach out to touch her as the shots rang-out and three bodies lay twitching with their throats rattling in the muddy, dirty, gravel car park. The shots were fast and furious, reminiscent of a Vietnam War movie. The cordite lay heavy in the air. The sound was the unmistakable report of the AKM and Pat came walking from the shadows.

"You took your time."
"Get the money and the coke and let's fuck-off," said Pat as he jumped into the back seat of the Granada.

18

10 Months Later

Almost a year had passed since the explosion, Simone's heart was broken for her lost sister; life just wasn't the same. It used to be routine to call Julie at certain times: 11.30am, when Simone would come back from the Gym; the first thing was to call her twin, sometimes it was for lunch, sometimes just for a talk and a laugh. Then at 4.00pm after she had collected the twins from school, another call to Julie; infact that was how they spent most of their lives, always in touch. Even when Julie was in Boston, the calls were always made. Their parents went ballistic over the collect-call bills, and now they were no more.

The press had done a good job of blackening Julie's name. All sorts of stories were being told about her. How she had joined the Republican movement while studying in the USA, they even nicknamed her 'The Black Widow' after the only property of her's that had been recovered from Belfast; a black dress and one red shoe that Simone didn't recognise. 'These people must have really got into her head,' thought Simone, 'she was so secretive, never expressed any political views; the press called her 'a sleeper'. The IRA had denied Julie and Conor were members of their organisation; but was not that just par-for-the-course with them? Mum and Dad are devastated; but the shame they're feeling.'

People had tried to console them, but they felt that it was false; they felt outcasts. Granny and Granddad Murphy didn't really know the twins that well. They had visited during school holidays; they loved them but didn't really know them. Granny Murphy felt pain for her son's loss. Granddad Murphy was proud and talked with his friends 'of the great deeds done by his revolutionary Granddaughter in her fight for Irish freedom', in the pubs of Cork.

It was June 4th, Simone and Julie's birthday; they would have been twenty-eight. Simone cried into her coffee as Frank handed her, her mail.

"Happy Birthday love." He put his arm around her as he sat on the bed. "There's a card there from the twins, they made it for you at school."
"They're so sweet," sobbed Simone, "I'm sorry you had to bring them to school today love, I just didn't feel up to it."
"That's OK Babe, that's why I took the day off. Maybe we can do something nice later on. My mum can pick up the kids from school."
"Oh I don't know love, I don't..."
"Simone I know it's really hard, but it's been nearly a year now, you have to think of me and the kids."
"*I try my best!*" Simone snapped. "I can't believe all these lies, my sister would never have been involved in all that."

"I know babe." Frank gave her a hug. "It will pass, are you going to open your cards?"
"I don't want to."
"Come on."

The first card was a large, padded one. 'To my wife on her Birthday.' Simone kissed Frank. Then a pink card with flowers drawn on, from the twins. "Ahh!" They both smiled. Frank's parents, Mum and Dad, and one from Granny and Granddad Murphy back in Ireland, then a little lilac coloured envelope with a strange post-mark in handwriting that looked all too familiar and sent a shiver down Simone's spine when she saw it.

"Frank!" Said Simone as she stared at the envelope. "Aruba! That's in the Caribbean isn't it?"
"Open it Simone."

Her eyes were wide and her hands were shaking as she gingerly took the card from the envelope. It had no signature but Simone screamed with delight as she threw the card in the air. She jumped off the bed and Frank caught her. They danced and kissed deeply before falling back on the bed.
"Frank did you see it?"
"Yes Babe." He put his finger to his lips as the card landed, open, on the bedside cabinet.

Happy Birthday Twin

Serendipity

xxx

EPILOGUE

Julie lay by the pool sipping a long Pinacolada, the sun blistering through the palm-trees as a cooling sea-breeze only sometimes caught a leaf and cast an ever-so-slight shadow on her perfectly tanned legs, that seemed to go on for ever. A high-cut bikini and tiny waistline gave pride of place to a diamond navel-ring. The bow she had tied at the back of her neck was under constant pressure to hold back her cleavage. Her left breast partially covered by a few strands of her raven hair. Her deep blue eyes were hidden behind designer shades.

"Is this bed taken?" A German woman blocked out the sun as she tried to place a towel on a sun-lounger that lay empty, except for a set of Oakley sunglasses and a little hip-bag that contained some tanning oil and a lip balm.
"Yes one of the boys is using that." She nodded towards Conor and Pat.

Conor had a diving mask around his neck. His tan not yet complete still showed a little red around the shoulders. Pat being fair-skinned was burnt. Pat smiled back at Mary, who's bleach-blond hair was due a refit. The chlorine was giving her a hairdo any Star Trek fan would have been proud of; green. Mary's bikini was under no pressure: she sunbathed topless. She loved the glances and the bickering 'they' caused when couples passed. She winked at Julie as girls scolded their boyfriends.

Four Spanish tourists were trying hard to catch every word Pat spoke as bubbles streamed from the mouthpiece of one of their bottles of air.

"They're teaching scuba." said Mary. An ice-cold drop of coconut milk hit her tummy like a teardrop exploding, the creamy white spreading out fast like a tiny oil slick on top of her tanning-oil.

"Ya." The German woman muttered something in her native tongue as she stomped away; her feet splashing in the poolside water.

"Are you nearly finished boys?" Mary called wiping the splash from her tummy. Her fingers with perfectly manicured nails, subconsciously making sure, that fresh paint stayed untouched; she took another sip.
"Two minutes girls." Conor smiled at them as he cleared his mask.
"You should come in the water and try this girls." said Pat as he lifted the bottles of air from the pool and stacked them neatly in a row.
"Maybe tomorrow," said Julie, as she threw them towels and took another sip of her drink.
"Graciãs. Adios." The Spanish people waved as they left the pool.

"Thanks for taking that class for me Pat, we were so busy today." The boys knew Nadia, the diving instructor, from a previous trip. A pretty girl, slim with an athletic figure, in her mid-twenties, with mousy-brown hair and a cheeky smile. She handed Pat a pass for free dives,

somewhat underhandedly with her left hand and a little 'don't-tell' wink and took the mask with her right hand.
"No problem, I enjoyed it, it was like teaching back in my army days." He gave the pass to Mary for safekeeping.
"And what about you girls, when are you coming for a dive?" She teased in her French-Canadian accent.
"We'll see." Julie blushed. Conor went to the bar.

Dinner that night was in a hotel restaurant. There were three, Caribbean, Chinese and Italian. Conor was pretending to be Don Corlione as he ordered.

"Great this ain't it Pat?"
"Yeah, that few quid goes a long way out here. And sure we're living like kings with our two queens." He lifted his wineglass as if to toast. The two girls looked at each other; they had heard it all before.

"Flattery will get you everywhere," said Mary, "so get another round in." They all laughed.
"Pat," said Conor, "nigh we're all together."
"Yeah?"
"What exactly did happen that night in Dublin?"
"Nah Conor," he shook his head, "not much. I'll tell you some time over a pint."
"What?" said Julie. "After all we've been through, you'd better tell us."
"Come on," said Mary. A sly smirk came on Pat's face and he started.

"...So you can picture the scene; Bunny's lying there bollock-naked on the floor."
"She's a girl Pat." said Julie.

"OK, butt-naked. I'm standing there with a hard-on and a two-inch blade stuck in my leg."

"What one was the biggest Pat? Said Conor, the girls laughed.

"Do you want to hear this story or what?"

"Sorry, carry on."

"And that fat bastard, Ginty, standing there with the AK, I nearly shit myself."

"What he do? Asked Conor.

"Fuck all. I jumped on him."

"Did you pull your trousers up?"

"No I didn't, I had no time, I thought he was about to blow my head off."

"So what happened?"

"If anyone had seen us they would have thought Ginty was rootin' the two of us. Bunny lying there, naked to the world and me with me trousers round me ankles tryin' to push some fat bastard with a rifle off me."

"So how'd he get shot then?"

"He didn't."

"What?"

"He didn't, there were no bullets in the magazine."

"What?" They all said together.

"They were in the grip-bag. He was going to beat me with the rifle."

"I don't believe you Pat," said Conor, but he did really.

"Swear to fuck. He ended up on top of me with the rifle across my throat; I thought I was going to choke to death."

"So what did you do?" The girls were engrossed.

"I grabbed him by the balls and he screamed like a fat pig."

"So how come the news said he was shot?"

"Well I got the rifle off him and got on my feet, I gave him two or three cracks with the butt to knock him out, but I may have hit him a wee bit too hard." Pat laughed.

"And what did she do?"

"She was laughing like fuck, she was out of her head."

"And what did you do? asked Conor.

"What do you think I done? I gathered everything up and got Bunny by the arm and fucked off to a hotel."

"You what!"

"Aye, we didn't think he was dead. He was still making noises when Bunny was pulling her jeans on and taking the crack out of his pockets."

"You mad bastard."

"I swear I didn't mean to kill him. I've known him a long time, but fuck him now anyway."

"What did you bring her with you for?" asked Mary.

"To shag her. I was gagging."

"You dirty bastard!" said Mary. Conor was laughing.

"There must have been a couple of bullets dropped out of the bag, that's why the news said, 'believed to be gunshot wounds.' "

"And what was Bunny like?" asked Conor. "Was she any good?"

"Beautiful kid. Far better than Pam and her five sisters."

"Dirty Pig!" said Mary.

"Now that was before I met you love," giggled Pat.

"Then what happened?" asked Conor.

"Well the next thing I know, I was standing in the corridor of the Europa hotel and you were trying to stab me with a knife."

All rights to this publication are reserved. No part, howsoever presented, may be reproduced in any form or by any means without prior permission being obtained by the author or his appointed agents being the owners of this and related intellectual property.

I would like to thank my nephew Antóin Currie for his help in publishing this story, without your help and your patience this would never have happened.

INSPIRATION

I always, as a child, wanted to write stories. I was good at 'telling' stories; I just did not know how to express myself with the written word.

Well I could; maybe I just didn't have the confidence.

I wrote a story about an incident I was involved in, as a teenager, and thought it was good, I just needed some encouragement; it wasn't forthcoming in Belfast in the 1970s.

As part of the school curriculum, I read Shane, The Call of The Wild, Tom Sawyer and Of Mice and Men. These books were read with the class and I was more into the stories than how they were written.

I never read when I left school as I was too busy with work. Bars served me, girls started to notice me and Sky TV had started. All those new channels!…Drugs raised it's ugly head and the easy money, well I say *easy* very flippantly as it was the hardest money I ever earned, what with people trying to kill me or put me in prison and it's even harder to hold on to as you just keep buying nice things. Then I came to prison.

I had watched 'The Exorcist' movie as a young adult and thought it was great. People would tell me that the book was better, but being an Irish Catholic, if I had brought a copy of the book or film into the house; my mum would have went crazy! In my mothers' eyes, it would have been tantamount to inviting Satan into the home.

So whilst in the library of HMP Leyhill, quite by chance, I stumbled across, 'The Exorcist.'

As I remember it, the opening paragraph goes something like this.

"Like the brief, doomed flare of exploding suns that register dimly upon blind men's eyes, the beginning of the horror passed almost unnoticed."

WOW! I was hooked. Mr Blatty had me hook, line and sinker! I thought about that paragraph for a long time, what kind of an imagination could think of that? Brilliant! I kept squeezing my eyelids together as hard as I could to get the effect. Brilliant!

As I read on, I could almost feel the complex workings of the mind of Peter William Blatty.

Blatty describes the approach of Karl, the servant, (and again I'm paraphrasing as I can't directly quote the book from memory), as "a stocky man with pieces of tissue stuck to his face where he had cut himself shaving. He stood at the table, breathing."

He describes the drawing room with words such as "smells of coffee, furniture polish and of secrets between rich uncles."

When I had finished the book, I knew I had to put down, on paper, the stories I had been telling.

Depending on how you look at them, some of my stories could be frightening, but they weren't 'horror.' Some were quite funny and some, I think are just *lies*. *STORIES*. So I needed to read a different genre, something close to what I wanted to write.

My first efforts at writing were stories of my childhood and early adult life, true life stories; I thought they were good, so I let some of the men read them. This guy, who worked in the library of HMP Hewell Grange (where I had moved to), and would tell anyone who would listen that he had 'three degrees.' So that became his name, 'The Three Degrees,' said to me. "You write like Roddy Doyle."

I'm ashamed to say, but I didn't know who Roddy Doyle was. I got one of his books and loved it. An Irish writer, writing about life in Dublin. Coming from Belfast, I could relate to it, how he used Irish terminology. That's how I would write my stories, in my own colloquial dialect.

My story was going to be a thriller, so I needed a bit more guidance and James Bond just wasn't going to cut it! 'Shaken, not stirred,' were not the words I was looking for. Nor, for that matter, were they used much on the streets of Belfast, (not in public anyway), unless you were talking about a petrol bomb!

So my author of choice was ex SAS man, Andy McNab. He had been to Belfast. He was from the real world. Let's have a look at his work.

I didn't read his first book as it was a true account of his time during the Gulf War. I got his first novel and loved it. In fact, I read every novel of his that the library had.

I must admit that Roddy Doyle did inspire me to write 'my version' of one of his sex scenes, and maybe I had an idea from Mr Blatty and Mr McNab. *I was only learning from the masters!* Three great writers who gave me great inspiration.

That's about all the training I had before I wrote my own little novel. Koestler Outstanding Award Winner 2003. 'The Secret.'

As aforementioned, I had moved from Leyhill to Hewell Grange and whilst doing my induction, I met Sally, the Head Teacher. I explained that I would love to do some creative writing and asked if the Education Department had such a course.

Sally told me it didn't but said that there was a lovely teacher by the name of Chris Fone and she would love to work with me on a writing project. So I signed up for education.

I was mainly writing poems and little stories, as well as reading my books for inspiration and as part of the course I had to do English and Maths exams. One of the exams needed a story, so I wrote about a friend of mine, Conor Loughlin.

Conor had an older brother called Micky who had been my best friend back in Belfast. Micky and I had been involved in boxing and kick-boxing and had fought on the same bill lots of times. We had even dated two friends. Micky's long term relationship had broken up, so he left Belfast to live on the Isle of Wight and start a new life. This left Conor at a loss and, being as good as a brother to him, I took him under my wing.

Conor was only seventeen and I was twenty eight, so when he came out to the 'discos' in the working men's clubs of Ardoyne with me and my friends, he was out with the 'big lads.' He didn't even drink!

As the lads do, we all eyed up the girls, 'the local talent.' Conor, wanting to be 'one of the boys,' would say, as girls passed, "I had her last week." This went on for a while so we grilled him, put him under lots of pressure and got to the truth. 'HAD' meant 'danced with' in the 17 year old mind of Conor Loughlin. By the end of the night Conor admitted that he was a virgin; and that's where Julie Murphy comes in.

Julie was a friend of mine and my girlfriend, Lisa Irvine. These girls could have passed for sisters and were the personification of my fictional characters, Julie and Simone. (Well they were actually based on Lisa as she had been my girl).

When I describe Julie, I'm describing Lisa as a twenty six year old and when I describe Mary wearing the black wig, I'm describing Lisa as a twenty year old, the first time I met her, in the street, outside her family home.

She looked so beautiful and I fancied her! She played it really cool with me; it was a few years before we got together.

Conor was a good looking lad, and when I told Julie he was a virgin, she was on him like a pit-bull on a cat.

'And in the morning the boy became a man.'

Mary McAuley. I have had two girlfriends named Mary McAuley. I have used this name as both these ladies have played an important part in my life. ***Two beautiful women who were never prostitutes!***

At the start of my prison sentence I met a man from Dublin, Pat Gorman. He was an ex Irish solider, had served in Beirut with the NATO forces and had a few stories of his own. He ended up in prison in England for doing something stupid when he was drunk, he was a good lad and we formed a good friendship.

I got my category D status, which is the lowest security risk, and moved to open conditions. After a while, I received two letters. I recognised one, as I knew Pat Gormans' handwriting. The other I didn't recognise so I read Pats' first.

Pat told me that he had met a Belfast lad who knew me. Pat had moved prisons also, to a C-Cat somewhere in the country, and the lads name was Conor Loughlin. I immediately opened the other letter, as they were in the same kind of envelope and it was from Conor Loughlin.

Conor told me that he had come to England, got involved with the supply of drugs and ended up with a six stretch for the 'social supply of,' whatever that means.

He told me that he had been in a half-way house and had formed an *'improper relationship'* with a female member of staff. I got all the gory details. He told someone, the *secret* got out, she got sacked and he got moved back to closed conditions. This was the story I used for my English exam.

Chris Fone planted the seed. She asked me. "How could you develop this story Tommy?" So I started to think.

I had all these stories, of my own, that I wanted to write about, but each story, by itself, could have been told in a few hundred words and events I had witnessed through the 'Troubles' in Belfast, were what I wanted to write about. I knew I couldn't write about specific events, as everyone has their own interpretation of those, but I thought that I could use things that I had witnessed, change them, spin them and fit them into a fictional story. That is what I did.

I didn't plan how I was going to write the story, I just went with it. In fact that's how I still write. Most of the time on the project is spent thinking, then I just grab a pen and write down my thoughts and dreams.

As I couldn't use, nor did not know the girls name who got sacked, I thought I would use the name of Julie

Murphy as the principal female. She had been Conors first conquest (ah that should be the other way round) and they did meet in such extraordinary circumstances…

I started the first paragraph…Conor walked the corridor… I didn't know it at the time that that was in the third person, and that's how the main body of the story went. After I had finished the story I still had one more little story that I wanted to put in, I just didn't know how to.

This story was of a Belfast street riot in Turf Lodge, where I had grown up. It involved these two little kids who I *knew* very well, in fact you would have thought one of them was my twin. I knew this story off by heart and it had to go in.

My thoughts were to write it as the little kid (they were 14) would write it himself right after the event, I didn't know either that this was in the 'first person,' but how could I fit it in? Then I remembered 'The Exorcist,' it had a prologue, so that's how I would do it, write it as a prologue set in 1974, the year Conor was born, to let the reader know what kind of world Conor was born into. It worked.

I wrote almost 42,000 words, which just about made it a novel, I think 30 or 35,000 is a novella, and off it was sent to the Koestler Awards where it won the Random House Outstanding Award for Prose. It's now called the Platinum Award. This was in 2003.

I received £100 prize money and donated it to Birmingham Children's Hospital.

Thanks to

My dad Francie who died in 2007; he would have loved this story, I think I got my imagination from him, I miss you da.

Heart felt love to my mum Sadie; thank you mammy for always being there; you were my rock through dark days.

To my sister Jacqui who *forced and bullied* me to remove the 'C' word; ah well I replaced them, all but one, and that one is staying.

My sister Rose and brother-in-law Jim for their constant support and my brother Fra for being Fra.

I'd like to thank Mark and Keith for their help with the typing and Pete for the original artwork.

Terry Pegrum for his help with the editing and formatting; who did get his own way and thankfully this font.

Thanks to my friend John McMahon of The Craic magazine for his advice in the publication of this story.

And again to my nephew Antóin for his help in publishing the revised v2 version.

My heart and loyalty will always be with the people who stood by me through the hardest time in my life. They gave their friendship and support unconditionally and did not judge me. I met all of these people on or around 01/09/1997 when I opened my first business, The Lyndhurst Pub in Birmingham, and these people have been my friends ever since. To put their names down randomly may suggest a hierarchy or preference, so I shall use the method Mr Rolls and Mr Royce used, alphabetically.

Gez Gordon, Donald Nesbitt, Dee O'Rourke, Tom O'Rourke, Billy Shanahan, and Tom Shanahan.

Through my trials and tribulations, these people asked for or expected nothing from me, friendship kept them there and mine will always be with them.

The inspirational David Apparicio of The Chrysalis Programme for changing my thought process, teaching me to live in the gap and helping me with this massive paradigm shift.

And once again Tom O'Rourke, a man who has been with me 20 years, through thick and thin. Even as a lad he showed maturity and strength of character way beyond his years. Brothers.

Finally, I'd like to dedicate this piece of work to the memory of my dearest, darling friend Lisa Irvine who died suddenly, in 2013 at the age of 45.

Thank you Lisa, for spending some of your life with me. The memories will always be with me, the happy and the sad times but mostly the good times. I'll never forget you, my green eyed girl.

Rest in peace my darling.
Love
Tommy. X.

Congratulations dad.
Love
TJ
X
Contact Tommy at tommymcg50@hotmail.com

Printed in Great Britain
by Amazon